ANTONY AND CLEOPATRA

NOTES

including
- *Life of Shakespeare*
- *Brief Plot Synopsis*
- *List of Characters*
- *Summaries and Commentaries*
- *Character Analyses*
- *Questions for Review*
- *Selected Bibliography*

by
James F. Bellman, Jr., M.A.
and
Kathryn Bellman, M.A., J.D.
Department of English
University of Nebraska

Cliffs Notes

INCORPORATED

LINCOLN, NEBRASKA 68501

Editor

Gary Carey, M.A.
University of Colorado

Consulting Editor

James L. Roberts, Ph.D.
Department of English
University of Nebraska

Cliffs Notes, Inc.　　　Lincoln, Nebraska

ABS-6335

CONTENTS

CHARACTER ANALYSES

ANTONY AND CLEOPATRA NOTES

LIFE OF SHAKESPEARE

Many books have assembled facts, reasonable suppositions, traditions, and speculations concerning the life and career of William Shakespeare. Taken as a whole, these materials give a rather comprehensive picture of England's foremost dramatic poet. Tradition and sober supposition are not necessarily false because they lack proved bases for their existence. It is important, however, that persons interested in Shakespeare should distinguish between *facts* and *beliefs* about his life.

From one point of view, modern scholars are fortunate to know as much as they do about a man of middle-class origin who left a small English country town and embarked on a professional career in sixteenth-century London. From another point of view, they know surprisingly little about the writer who has continued to influence the English language and its drama and poetry for more than three hundred years. Sparse and scattered as these facts of his life are, they are sufficient to prove that a man from Stratford by the name of William Shakespeare wrote the major portion of the thirty-seven plays which scholars ascribe to him. The concise review which follows will concern itself with some of these records.

No one knows the exact date of William Shakespeare's birth. His baptism occurred on Wednesday, April 26, 1564. His father was John Shakespeare, tanner, glover, dealer in grain, and town official of Stratford; his mother, Mary, was the daughter of Robert Arden, a prosperous gentleman-farmer. The Shakespeares lived on Henley Street.

Under a bond dated November 28, 1582, William Shakespeare and Anne Hathaway entered into a marriage contract. The baptism of their eldest child, Susanna, took place in Stratford in May, 1583. One year and nine months later their twins, Hamnet and Judith, were christened in the same church. The parents named them for the poet's friends Hamnet and Judith Sadler.

Early in 1596, William Shakespeare, in his father's name, applied to the College of Heralds for a coat of arms. Although positive proof is lacking, there is reason to believe that the Heralds granted this request, for in 1599 Shakespeare again made application for the right to quarter his coat of arms with that of his mother. Entitled to her father's coat of arms, Mary had lost this privilege when she married John Shakespeare before he held the official status of gentleman.

In May of 1597, Shakespeare purchased New Place, the outstanding residential property in Stratford at that time. Since John Shakespeare had suffered financial reverses prior to this date, William must have achieved success for himself.

Court records show that in 1601 or 1602, William Shakespeare began rooming in the household of Christopher Mountjoy in London. Subsequent disputes between Shakespeare's landlord, Mountjoy, and his son-in-law, Stephen Belott, over Stephen's wedding settlement led to a series of legal actions, and in 1612 the court scribe recorded Shakespeare's deposition of testimony relating to the case.

In July, 1605, William Shakespeare paid four hundred and forty pounds for the lease of a large portion of the tithes on certain real estate in and near Stratford. This was an arrangement whereby Shakespeare purchased half the annual tithes, or taxes, on certain agricultural products from sections of land in and near Stratford. In addition to receiving approximately ten percent income on his investment, he almost doubled his capital. This was possibly the most important and successful investment of his lifetime, and it paid a steady income for many years.

Shakespeare is next mentioned when John Combe, a resident of Stratford, died on July 12, 1614. To his friend, Combe bequeathed the sum of five pounds. These records and similar ones are important, not because of their economic significance but because they prove the existence of a William Shakespeare in Stratford and in London during this period.

On March 25, 1616, William Shakespeare revised his last will and testament. He died on April 23 of the same year. His body lies within the chancel and before the altar of the Stratford church. A rather wry inscription is carved upon his tombstone:

Good Friend, for Jesus' sake, forbear
To dig the dust enclosed here;
Blest be the man that spares these stones
And curst be he that moves my bones.

The last direct descendant of William Shakespeare was his grand-daughter, Elizabeth Hall, who died in 1670.

These are the most outstanding facts about Shakespeare the man, as apart from those about the dramatist and poet. Such pieces of information, scattered from 1564 through 1616, declare the existence of such a person, not as a writer or actor, but as a private citizen. It is illogical to think that anyone would or could have fabricated these details for the purpose of deceiving later generations.

In similar fashion, the evidence establishing William Shakespeare as the foremost playwright of his day is positive and persuasive. Robert Greene's *Groatsworth of Wit*, in which he attacked Shakespeare, a mere actor, for presuming to write plays in competition with Greene and his fellow playwrights, was entered in the *Stationers' Register* on September 20, 1592. In 1594 Shakespeare acted before Queen Elizabeth, and in 1594 and 1595 his name appeared as one of the shareholders of the Lord Chamberlain's Company. Francis Meres in his *Palladis Tamia* (1598) called Shakespeare "mellifluous and hony-tongued" and compared his comedies and tragedies with those of Plautus and Seneca in excellence.

Shakespeare's continued association with Burbage's company is equally definite. His name appears as one of the owners of the Globe in 1599. On May 19, 1603, he and his fellow actors received a patent from James I designating them as the King's Men and making them Grooms of the Chamber. Late in 1608 or early in 1609, Shakespeare and his colleagues purchased the Blackfriars Theatre and began using it as their winter location when weather made production at the Globe inconvenient.

Other specific allusions to Shakespeare, to his acting and his writing, occur in numerous places. Put together, they form irrefutable testimony that William Shakespeare of Stratford and London was the leader among Elizabethan playwrights.

One of the most impressive of all proofs of Shakespeare's authorship of his plays is the First Folio of 1623, with the dedicatory verse which appeared in it. John Heminge and Henry Condell, members of Shakespeare's own company, stated that they collected and issued the plays as a memorial to their fellow actor. Many contemporary poets contributed eulogies to Shakespeare; one of the best known of these poems is by Ben Jonson, a fellow actor and, later, a friendly rival. Jonson also criticized Shakespeare's dramatic work in *Timber: or, Discoveries* (1641).

Certainly there are many things about Shakespeare's genius and career which the most diligent scholars do not know and cannot explain, but the facts which do exist are sufficient to establish Shakespeare's identity as a man and his authorship of the thirty-seven plays which reputable critics acknowledge to be his.

BRIEF PLOT SYNOPSIS

ACT I

This act serves to introduce the main characters—Antony, Cleopatra, and Caesar; it also outlines the main forces which motivate each of them. The first scene is set in Alexandria, where two of Antony's men, Demetrius and Philo, describe the lovers' relationship. Caesar appears in a later scene, and we see how he perceives Antony and Cleopatra's relationship. In addition, his comments about Antony reveal a great deal about his own character. We also have ample evidence in this act that Antony and Cleopatra are deeply in love, but Antony does not realize the tragic possibilities of their infatuation, yet he is torn by divided loyalties. In short, this first act sets out what the relationships are among the main characters, and it establishes the basic conflicts that dominate the rest of the play: first, Antony and Cleopatra and their love for one another; and second, Antony's rivalry with Caesar.

ACT II

In this act, Shakespeare accelerates the inevitable final conflict between his primary characters. Pompey, an insurgent force against Rome, has become enough of a threat to the Roman Empire that the triumvirs are forced to form a truce in order to present a united front. Antony and Caesar decide to resolve the fighting among themselves; this new "alliance" is to be cemented by the marriage of Antony and Octavia, Caesar's sister. When Cleopatra finds out that Antony has married, she is devastated by the news. But she resolves not to give up Antony so easily. In the meantime, even while Antony pledges his loyalty to Octavia, his thoughts have returned to Egypt and Cleopatra.

ACT III

Most of the main events of the play have their beginnings in this act. It begins with the continued efforts on Antony's part to work on behalf of Rome and regain his stature in the world of politics and war. But before long, he tires of the pursuit of power in Rome and decides to return to Egypt.

Octavia accompanies Antony to Athens, but she returns to Rome alone after Antony decides to return to Cleopatra. Octavia's disgrace gives Caesar sufficient reason to hate Antony even more than he already does, and he vows revenge. Octavia's discovery that Antony is glorifying Cleopatra and her children, one of them the illegitimate son of Julius Caesar, provides enough of an excuse for Caesar to declare that both Antony and Cleopatra are traitors. War begins, and Antony's forces are defeated; the rest of the play focuses, thus, on the aftermath of this battle and its effect on the love between Antony and Cleopatra.

ACT IV

Antony is at first despondent over his defeat. He places the blame on Cleopatra, who fled with her ships. He jeers that she will desert him for Caesar, just as some of his troops already have. She convinces him that he is wrong, and they courageously make one last attempt to defeat Caesar. They win a battle, but their victory is short-lived, and finally they are absolutely defeated. Again, Antony doubts Cleopatra's loyalty, and so she flees to her monument, the tomb where her body is to be buried after her death. She hopes to make Antony see the error of his doubts about her by sending him word that she is dead. Antony suffers great remorse and falls upon his sword. He does not die immediately, however, and he is taken to the monument, where Cleopatra is waiting for him. They spend his final moments together, and Cleopatra is left to face the Romans alone.

ACT V

This final act concentrates on Cleopatra's last hours, as she negotiates with the Roman victors. Caesar has promised that she will be treated with honor in Rome, but she has good reason not to believe him. One of Caesar's officers, Dolabella, warns her not to put her faith in Caesar's promises. Cleopatra resolves to die rather than be taken captive to Rome, and she and her women have a basket of poisonous snakes smuggled to them in order to commit suicide. Thus, both Antony and Cleopatra die and they ultimately deprive Caesar's final victory of its full glory, as he finally acknowledges.

LIST OF CHARACTERS

Mark Antony

A middle-aged Roman general who rules the Roman Empire along with Lepidus and Octavius Caesar. He is torn between his desire for Cleopatra and the demands of his position as a world ruler.

Octavius Caesar

The adopted son of Julius Caesar, his grand-uncle, he is only in his early twenties, but he is determined to ultimately be the sole ruler of the Roman Empire.

Lepidus

As a member of the Triumvirate, he serves as a mediator between Antony and Caesar, the two rivals; he has no real power of his own.

Cleopatra

She is aware of her duties as Queen of Egypt, but she is deeply infatuated with Antony; her heroic courage is revealed when she and Antony are defeated and she chooses to die in Egypt, rather than return to Rome as a captive.

Octavia

She becomes engaged to Antony in order to cement a political and military truce between Antony and her brother, Caesar.

Sextus Pompeius (Pompey)

Formerly a Roman, Pompey left Rome with a faction that included several pirates and some of Julius Caesar's navy. He attempted to form his own kingdom, and he is able to cause the Triumvirate trouble by plundering their ships.

Enobarbus

Antony's trusted lieutenant and close friend; eventually, he deserts the man he both admires and pokes fun at, yet he later commits suicide in remorse.

Ventidius

Another of Antony's officers, he is sent to fight the Parthians. He is a brave and capable general and is absolutely loyal to Antony.

Scarus

Another of Antony's officers; he serves as Antony's aide after Enobarbus deserts his general.

Dercetas

He is one of the first to find Antony after Antony has tried to kill himself. Dercetas deserts to Caesar's faction, taking Antony's sword as a sign that the enemy is almost defeated.

Demetrius and Philo

These friends of Antony's are among those who go with him to Egypt. They long to see their general as he was before he fell in love and forgot about his political and military duties.

Canidius

He is a Lieutenant General to Antony, but he deserts Antony's camp for Caesar's faction after Antony's first major defeat.

Euphronius

He serves as an ambassador from Antony to Caesar.

Fulvia

She does not appear in the play, but she is Antony's first wife.

Taurus

As Lieutenant General to Caesar, his strategies help Caesar to win the war against the forces of Antony and Cleopatra.

Maecenas

An officer and a friend of Caesar; when the triumvirs meet at the house of Lepidus in Rome to effect a truce, Maecenas is present.

Agrippa

Another friend of Caesar; along with Maecenas, he never judges Antony quite as lightly as does his general.

Proculeius

This friend of Caesar acts as a messenger and tells Cleopatra on behalf of Caesar that she need not be afraid for her welfare.

Dolabella

Unlike Proculeius, Dolabella feels pity for Cleopatra and warns her that Caesar's promises to her may be empty ones.

Thyreus

He also acts as a messenger, telling Cleopatra of Antony's defeat and Octavius's victory.

Charmian

She is one of Cleopatra's closest friends and court confidantes.

Iras

Another of Cleopatra's attendants.

Alexas

A servant of Cleopatra who acts as a messenger between her and Antony.

Mardian

This member of Cleopatra's entourage is a eunuch, a fact which Cleopatra enjoys teasing him about.

Menas

A pirate; he advises Pompey to take the triumvirs captive and have them murdered while they are attending a banquet aboard his ship.

Menecrates

As a chief officer of Pompey, he helps his general plan strategies.

Varrius

He is warlike and ambitious, like Pompey, but he is less unscrupulous than Menas.

Eros and Gallus

Eros is a friend of Antony's; Gallus is a friend of Caesar's.

Silius

An officer in Ventidius's army.

Seleucus and Diomedes

Attendants to Cleopatra.

A Soothsayer

A fortuneteller who tells Charmian that she will outlive Cleopatra.

SUMMARIES AND COMMENTARIES

ACT I – SCENE 1

Summary

The play opens in Alexandria, in one of the rooms of Cleopatra's palace. Two of Antony's friends, Demetrius and Philo, are discussing

Antony's increasing fondness for Cleopatra. Philo, in particular, is worried about "this dotage" that his general has for the Egyptian queen; to him, Antony's passion "o'erflows the measure." He feels that a general's passion is best spent on the battlefield "in the scuffles of great fights." As they ponder their general's unreasonable behavior, there is a fanfare of trumpets, and Antony and Cleopatra enter, accompanied by the queen's ladies-in-waiting and her attendant eunuchs. Philo is fearful that all this pomp and beauty has turned his general from a fierce warrior into an addled lover. Significantly, he worries that Antony, "the triple pillar of the world," has been translated into "a strumpet's fool."

Cleopatra's first words to Antony are teasing. She wants to know how much Antony loves her, and he boasts that if any love can be measured, then it is poor love indeed ("There's beggary in the love that can be reckoned"). But Cleopatra tantalizes him for still more compliments—more verbal proof of his love. Foolishly, he tries to appease her.

They are interrupted by a messenger who has brought news from Rome, but Antony clearly is in no mood to hear or discuss military matters. All of his thoughts are on his beloved Cleopatra, who mocks the messenger's urgency; she sarcastically jests that Caesar is probably sending yet another order to "do this, or this;/ Take in that kingdom. . . ." Games of war bore her; she delights in equating the taking of whole kingdoms to being no more than a mere daily errand, ordered by the "scarce-bearded Caesar."

The Queen's strategy works; Antony is furious that *anyone* would interrupt his thoughts and his time with his beloved Cleopatra. "Let Rome in [the] Tiber melt," he roars. The only "messenger" he will see is Cleopatra; his devotion to the worthy Cleopatra comprises "the nobleness of life." They exit with the queen's attendants, and Demetrius and Philo are left alone to ponder their general's transformation. Rumor has already reached Rome of Antony's romantic waywardness. Demetrius hopes that tomorrow he will once again see proof that his general is still "that great property."

Commentary

Shakespeare does not dally with theatrical conventions of lengthy exposition. Almost immediately we are introduced to the two lovers, who are clearly passionate lovers. There is only a modicum of introduction as the play opens. Briefly, two of Antony's friends discuss their general's infatuation with Cleopatra. They describe Antony as if he had undergone some strange sort of metamorphosis; it seems to them that his eyes, which once looked upon battlefields, "now bend, now turn/ The office and devotion of their view/ Upon a tawny front." His soldier's heart is no longer courageous; instead, it "reneges all temper/ And is become the bellows and the fan/ To cool a gypsy's lust."

After Antony and Cleopatra have made their entrance, it is clear that Antony has indeed let himself be seduced—body and soul—by Cleopatra's sensuality and charm. It is also clear that the Romans in general dislike Cleopatra, in spite of her legendary ability to enchant males—or perhaps because of it. This prejudiced view toward Cleopatra is developed throughout the play, but as we will see, Shakespeare was not content to present her as only a one-dimensional character; she is more than merely a sensual woman who happens to rule an entire country.

As Antony and Cleopatra talk, both of them use exaggerated language to swear that their love is greater than any other love in the world; their love, they believe, is more than this world can hold. This is not idle overstatement, for their intense love for one another will be the cause of their deaths. Time and again in the play this key idea will be emphasized: love and the worlds of politics and war belong in separate spheres and can never coalesce or merge. The central theme of this play is exactly that—love vs. war, and Shakespeare will weave this theme in and out of the action as the play progresses. By the end of the tragedy, it will seem as if the concept of war has won, but we should not be too hasty to come to that decision. Upon reflection, we will see that the final act of this play is ambiguous. It is possible that love may finally be the victor after all.

In this act, however, Shakespeare's emphasis is clearly on Antony's current displeasure with political matters. The messenger who has come with a letter from Rome gives Cleopatra a chance to tease Antony that he is dominated by Caesar, a much younger man. Her motive is to goad Antony into declaring his independence of Rome—and she succeeds, for Antony retorts that "kingdoms are clay; our dungy earth alike/ Feeds beast as man." Impetuously, he denies that Rome and the concerns of the political arena have any hold on him. Here, we should note his choice of words: Antony says that the earth is "dungy" and that kingdoms "melt" like mud into the rivers of the world. This comparison is ironically striking when we consider the "earthy" (sensual) interest for which he is forsaking Rome.

Antony thus reveals how malleable he really is, for Cleopatra clearly delights in toying with his vacillating passions. She teases him that since he has been unfaithful to his wife by becoming involved with her, it is quite likely that he will be unfaithful to her one day. Antony, of course, vehemently denies such a speculation. Here, he is willful and self-indulgent, and he is certainly fickle. We initially see him perhaps at his worst. Later, Shakespeare's dramatic portrait of him will be enlarged and will be developed in detail, stature, and complexity.

As for portraying Cleopatra, the Egyptian queen, Shakespeare remains faithful to the popular image of Cleopatra as the strumpet queen, so to speak, but he suggests that she, like Antony, is more complex than one might initially suppose. On one hand, she is a coquette who manipulates Antony so skillfully that he does what she wants. On the other, she emotionally needs to have Antony tell her how much he loves her; she needs to have him affirm for her that nothing else matters as much as their love. This clearly reveals a certain amount of insecurity on her part, and in that sense, it is quite possible that she has a genuine, if momentary, feeling of sympathy for Antony's wife; she can see herself in the same position – that is, Antony loves her now, but she can envision losing him later to another woman.

ACT I – SCENE 2

Summary

This scene also takes place in Cleopatra's palace in Alexandria. Cleopatra's servants are talking to a fortuneteller (a soothsayer) and are trying to get him to predict how they will all fare in love. Charmian and Iras, two of Cleopatra's attendants, and Alexas, one of her male attendants, are trying to get the soothsayer to specify their futures. He avoids direct answers, however, and instead, predicts that Charmian will outlive her mistress, Cleopatra. Enobarbus, a friend to Antony and an officer in his army (and also something of a cynic), is also present, and he interrupts the chatter of the servants when he hears someone coming. It is Cleopatra, looking for Antony. She says that Antony was mirthful until a "Roman thought" struck him and destroyed his happy mood.

Antony enters then, accompanied by a messenger, but Cleopatra and her attendants leave before he sees them. The messenger describes to Antony the outcome of a battle involving Antony's brother, Lucius, and Antony's wife, Fulvia, against Caesar. Lucius and Fulvia, formerly enemies, united forces in order to defeat Caesar, but failed.

The messenger has more to say, but he hesitates to speak plainly. Antony assures him that he need not mince words and bids him to give his message, even to the point of describing Cleopatra as she is talked about in Rome (for this is why Antony thinks that the messenger is hesitant): ". . . mince not the general tongue/ Name Cleopatra as she is call'd in Rome."

Another messenger enters and gives Antony a letter telling him that his wife, Fulvia, is dead and explaining what has happened. For a moment, Antony is overcome with remorse.

Enobarbus, Antony's lieutenant, enters then, and Antony tells him that they must prepare to leave for Rome. Enobarbus quips that if they leave, all the women will suffer and perhaps die from their absence. Antony, however, appears determined to forsake all of the enchantments of Egypt and return home. Enobarbus, at first, cannot imagine why Antony has had such a sudden change of heart, but then Antony reveals to him that Fulvia is dead.

Still, however, Enobarbus looks upon the whole matter rather cynically and tells Antony not to feel so bad; after all, Antony lost a wife he didn't want, and he now has a lover whom he does want: "This grief is crowned with consolation; your old smock brings forth a new petticoat." Enobarbus's comments, however, are ill-timed, for Antony is no longer in his usual devil-may-care mood, and he does not take Fulvia's death as lightly as his earlier behavior had led Enobarbus to expect: "No more light answers," Antony says, as he refuses to let his friend treat Fulvia's death flippantly. Furthermore, these events serve to remind Antony not to neglect his duties entirely. He resolves to return to Rome and see to business. For the time being, he must give up the pleasures of Egypt.

Commentary

Scene 2 introduces us to some of the minor characters, and it also includes a conversation about the nature of love. Thus, the main theme of the play remains in the foreground. The servants' witty, if somewhat cynical, treatment of the subject of love contrasts considerably with the exalted declarations of love that were made in the opening scene. An additional touch of dramatic irony is added when Charmian is exceedingly pleased at the idea that she will live longer than her mistress; little does she realize that her mistress will soon be dead.

Cleopatra's troubled comments about Antony's change of mood are characterized by her reference to Antony's "Roman thought." In Elizabethan times, the term "Roman" was often used because it was believed that the Romans as a nation were typically serious and devoted to duty (the theme of Virgil's *Aeneid*); thus, here, Cleopatra may be suggesting that Antony's thought was consistent with that sort of character; another possibility is that Antony was reminded of business which had to do with Rome—that is, his thoughts were about Rome; he literally had a "Roman thought."

Antony's demeanor is changed upon learning of the death of his wife, Fulvia. Immediately, he regrets that he once wished for her death. He sorrowfully remarks, "There's a great spirit gone!" Antony's guilt, to some extent, appears to spur his resolve to leave Egypt and return to Rome. When Enobarbus cynically comments upon the effect which their departure will have upon the women, Antony is not amused, and in contrast with his earlier speeches, where he seemed to be prepared to give up everything for the sake of love, he now seems quite willing to do just the opposite. Antony does not fear that Cleopatra will "die"; she is cunning, he says, echoing Enobarbus's comment that he has seen "her die twenty times upon far poorer moment" (for Shakespeare's audience, this allusion to dying possibly refers to the ecstasies of love, the moment of sexual climax which the Elizabethans often poetically likened to death).

In conclusion, Scene 2 basically shows the conflicting desires that struggle for dominance within Antony. He feels torn between his duties at home and his love for the Egyptian queen, and worse, he believes that he will never be able to reconcile these two passions. Yet he knows that, ultimately, he must choose one or the other. We also see contrasted in this scene the frivolity and the sensuality of life in Egypt, as typified by the games played by the servants with the soothsayer, and, in addition, we glimpse the troubled and serious world of the Romans, dominated by politics, not by love. Antony, too, senses the contrast, making plausible his sudden resolve to return to Rome and to more important matters.

ACT I – SCENE 3

Summary

The scene opens with Cleopatra instructing her attendants, Charmian, Alexas, and Iras, to aid her in a plan. They are to find Antony and observe what sort of mood he is in. If he seems to be happy, they are to tell him that Cleopatra is ill. But if he seems sad or moody, on the other hand, they are to tell him that she is "dancing." Presumably, her purpose is to make Antony feel guilty about being away from her; she wants to make him think about her – anything to draw his attention to her. It is a transparent and childish device, more typical of an adolescent than of a woman deeply in love.

Antony enters and wants to tell Cleopatra the sad news of Fulvia's death. However, Cleopatra is so involved in the game that she is playing that she doesn't notice that Antony is trying to tell her something important. He keeps trying to interrupt her egotistical monologue, but he cannot manage to communicate his sorrow. First, Cleopatra feigns illness, but when she sees that Antony doesn't notice, she begins berating him for his faithlessness. After a good deal of melodramatic emoting from Cleopatra, Antony is finally able to tell her that he must leave immediately. She is caught off-guard and is so distraught that he plans to leave so quickly that she accuses him of playacting. She accuses him further of being as false to her as he is false to Fulvia. At this point, Antony is finally able to tell her that Fulvia is dead.

This announcement, however, does not have the expected effect on Cleopatra. She merely retorts, selfishly, "Now I see, I see/ In Fulvia's death, how mine receiv'd shall be." But Antony is not moved by her childish histrionics, and he repeats that he must return to Rome.

Cleopatra continues to goad Antony, but to no effect. She repeats the charge that he is an excellent actor and that he plays well the role of an irritated, angry man. He answers Cleopatra that her own show of grief at his leaving might also be merely an act. She vows that her love for him is real and that her pain is as real as the pain of a woman in labor. Finally, it seems, she realizes that Antony's emotions may be genuine, and she also seems to realize that the quality of love is something that a person must take on faith. When the scene ends, Cleopatra is reconciled to the fact that Antony must leave, and thus they separate and swear vows of fidelity.

Commentary

Several themes are developed here. Once again, we see Cleopatra in a rather unfavorable light. She still seems to be more of a scheming coquette than a woman who loves Antony sincerely. Yet Cleopatra's insecurity, her constant comparing of her own situation with that of Fulvia, could also be interpreted to mean that she does love Antony a great deal and fears to lose him.

If this scene could be said to have one basic focus, it probably centers on acting and the theater—illusion as opposed to the real world. The second half of the scene, in particular, with its many references to acting, echoes the actual "staged scene" that we saw in the first half—that is, when Cleopatra instructed her servants to encourage Antony to worry about her and thus attract his attention. It is ironic that it is Cleopatra who accuses Antony of only *acting* as if he loves her; significantly, it was she, not he, who planned the earlier scenario with her servants. She herself "acts" according to plan when Antony enters, but her scheme fails when Antony refuses to humor her. As a result, they argue about whether or not their love is genuine.

The familiar Shakespearean theme of reality vs. illusion is paramount here. Egypt is a dream world, a world of romance and sensual delight, compared to Rome, a world of harsh reality, a world of politics and war. As a parallel, the relationship between Antony and Cleopatra exhibits dreamlike features, as well as serious sparring. Their love vacillates between a tawdry, superficial romance, a sort of romp in the garden of earthly delights, and a love that is sadder, a deeper kind of love that is more than sensual and may possibly survive the burdens placed on it by time and the world.

At this point, Shakespeare is still developing his theme of love and intrigue according to the popular ideas of his time concerning Antony and Cleopatra. Traditionally, these lovers have been presented as being entirely devoted to sensuality and self-gratification. Now, however, we see that while the faults of Shakespeare's hero and heroine are not entirely dispelled, the characters gain considerably in depth and humanity as the play progresses.

ACT I – SCENE 4

Summary

The scene now shifts to Rome and focuses on a discussion between Antony's co-triumvirs as they discuss the problems facing the empire. Here we have our first glimpse of Caesar Octavius and Lepidus. Although the subject of their discussion is Antony, their criticisms of him reveal a good deal about their own characters, not all of it praiseworthy.

Caesar enters reading a letter and is followed by Lepidus and their attendants. The two Romans catalogue Antony's faults ("he fishes, drinks, and wastes/ The lamps of night in revel"), and there is heavy irony in their apparent concession that Antony's activities might be acceptable under *other* circumstances. That is, Caesar says, "let's grant it is not/ Amiss to tumble on the bed of Ptolemy" (Cleopatra's former husband); of course, Julius Caesar, Octavius's uncle, enjoyed engaging in such sexual activities.

A messenger enters then with news from abroad: Pompey and two infamous pirates, Menecrates and Menas, are making "the sea serve them"; they have made "many hot inroads" into Italy, as well as creating havoc in the Mediterranean. Caesar uses this bad news as one more excuse to disparage Antony, who is conveniently absent and cannot defend himself. As an example of Antony's character, or lack of it, Caesar recalls an incident when Antony was "beaten from Modena," and not only was Antony defeated, but "famine did follow." Caesar also recalls that Antony escaped with his forces to the Alps, where he "didst drink/ The stale of horses and the gilded puddle/ Which beasts would cough at." Caesar is saddened: "It wounds thine honor . . ." he says, that Antony can now act so immaturely.

Commentary

Caesar admonishes Antony, the absent triumvir, to leave his "lascivious wassails [revels]" and to return to duty. He dwells on Antony's sensuality and his love of food and drink, and he hints further that Antony lacks character, for it is well known that in the difficult journey across the Alps, Antony would eat virtually anything rather than starve. Caesar cites the fact that Antony drank "gilded puddle" (animal urine) and "browsed on" (ate) tree bark rather than die in defeat. These acts of desperation, he says, suggest that Antony is a man of ignoble tastes, preferring as he does now the base pleasures of Egypt. Yet while it is true that Antony is a far more sensual and even a more self-indulgent man (in theory) than Caesar, the fact that Antony *could* and *did* survive the rigors of an Alpine winter attest to the fact that Antony has the prime virtues of strength and courage, regardless of whatever flaws of character that Caesar might accuse him of. Caesar, it should be noted, interprets Antony's character in the worst possible way. As a result, his attempt to turn these incidents into an indictment against Antony tells us, in reality, more about young Caesar's insecurities than it does about Antony. In the course of this play, we shall find that although Caesar is probably the more clever of the two men, Antony has a generosity of spirit that seldom permits him to level such abuses on Caesar and *his* excesses.

Interestingly, the scene ends as Caesar tells Lepidus that he is eager for the two of them to "show ourselves on the field"; he and Lepidus then pledge their loyalty to each other, echoing an earlier, similar pledge between Antony and Cleopatra in the previous scene.

ACT I – SCENE 5

Summary

Again we return to Alexandria; Cleopatra is in her palace with her attendants, Charmian and Iras, and Mardian, a eunuch. Now that Antony has departed, Cleopatra is at a loss for something to occupy her time. Primarily, she spends most of her time thinking of him and worrying about what he is doing; she seems to be more like a lovesick adolescent in this scene than the ruler of a great country.

She asks for mandragora, a sleeping potion, so that she can "sleep out this great gap of time [that] Antony is away."

She asks Mardian, perhaps only half-jokingly, if he has any "affections" or passionate feelings at all. He tells her that he does, although he can "do nothing"; yet, there *are* acts that he thinks about "fiercely." This is a play on words to some extent, for Cleopatra may be referring to any strong emotional feeling. Although Mardian's answer is ambiguous, one gets the impression that he is conscious of both meanings, and his answer seems to hint that although his sexual role in life is limited, he is as capable of passion and feeling as his mistress, Cleopatra, is.

Cleopatra then turns to Charmian and asks her to imagine what Antony is doing at this moment, how he looks, and what he is thinking. She can think of nothing that is not concerned with her love for Antony. She is about to swallow the "delicious poison" (her melodramatic term for the sleeping potion) when one of her servants, Alexas, enters with news of Antony. Cleopatra is delighted, and she tells Alexas that the mere fact that he has been near Antony makes him more precious in her eyes.

Alexas gives the Queen a pearl, a gift from Antony. It is a particularly valuable pearl for Alexas says that Antony kissed it; in fact, Antony bestowed upon it "many doubled kisses." In addition, Alexas says that Antony will "piece/ [Cleopatra's] throne with kingdoms. All the East . . . shall call her mistress." Cleopatra then eagerly questions Alexas about Antony: how he appeared and what sort of mood he was in. She also asks Alexas whether Antony seemed sad or merry, but Alexas quickly perceives that both potential responses could be wrong answers at this point; therefore, he diplomatically states that Antony seemed neither very sad nor very happy. This seems to satisfy Cleopatra, who would have been disturbed if Antony were distressed, but she would have been furious if he seemed *too* happy – without her. She then gives Alexas a message to deliver to Antony.

Cleopatra asks Charmian, as proof of Cleopatra's love for Antony, if she ever saw Cleopatra love Caesar (Julius Caesar, Octavius's adoptive father) so well. Charmian, not as clever nor as astute as Alexas in gauging Cleopatra's moods, gives an answer that praises Caesar. That is a mistake; Cleopatra wants unqualified assurance that she never loved *anyone* as much as she loves Antony;

she wants to hear it confirmed that every lover she had before Antony was a mere trifle, a flirtation. Only now has Cleopatra discovered true love. In response to Charmian's comment, Cleopatra orders Charmian *never* to compare Antony with Caesar again, nor even to suggest that they are equal in any way.

Commentary

This portrait of Cleopatra is, to a great extent, very much like her legendary reputation—that is, Cleopatra is a beautiful seductress, whose power to charm men is derived, in part, from her beauty and, in part, from her beguiling craftiness. Shakespeare doesn't deviate far from this characterization, one which was well known in his day. But beneath Cleopatra's whims and her girlish melodramatics over her absent lover, there is a hint that the very strength of her feeling portends a deeper affection than her behavior would indicate. It is as if adversity and tragedy must work their magic on this all-too-earthly pair before they and we, the audience, realize that the love which they profess may, in fact, be almost a supernatural love, a force ultimately more powerful to Antony than the fate of the Roman Empire itself.

ACT II – SCENE 1

Summary

In this scene, set in the insurrectionists' camp, Pompey (Sextus Pompeius), a rival general of the Triumvirate, plans his strategy with two of his officers, the sea pirates Menas and Menecrates. Pompey brags that he shall do well. Menas, however, is cautious and tells Pompey not to be overconfident, for Caesar and Lepidus are in the field and are prepared to fight and defend the empire. Pompey, however, rejects this news; he says, "I know they are in Rome together,/ Looking for Antony." Furthermore, he says that Cleopatra's wiles and her "Epicurean cooks [will so] sauce [Antony's] appetite" that Antony will be completely seduced by luxury that he will either forget about politics altogether or else he will be unable to defeat his enemies—if he finally does remember where his duty lies.

Varrius, an officer, enters bearing a message: Antony is expected to arrive in Rome momentarily, and, in fact, he has probably already arrived. This news disturbs Pompey, who now realizes that Antony may indeed be a threat. However, Pompey is not easily discouraged, and so he makes new plans. Menas suggests to Pompey that there is a weak link in the chain that forms the Triumvirate; a rumor persists that there is an enmity between Antony and Caesar. He also tells Pompey that Lucius Antony (Antony's brother) and Fulvia (Antony's late wife) joined forces against Caesar not long ago. Although it is doubted that Antony had anything to do with the attack, as he apparently didn't, perhaps there is some truth to the rumor that there are hard feelings within the Triumvirate. Pompey, of course, hopes that these alleged quarrels between Antony and Caesar will cause a sufficient rift, and that the Triumvirate will be weakened as a fighting force. Pompey can thus easily overwhelm them. However, Pompey is also aware of the possibility that the threat of an invasion from the outside will cause the Triumvirate to set aside their personal differences for the time being in order to meet with and oppose a common enemy. This is, in fact, what happens, at least for awhile.

Commentary

Pompey, an enemy of the Triumvirate which currently rules Rome, believes that his hold over that portion of the Mediterranean that he controls is increasing. He believes, moreover, that he is now in a position to challenge the empire with little threat from Antony, who appears to have forsaken politics for love. Pompey is convinced that Antony, an experienced soldier, is the only real obstacle in his quest for power, and now with Antony diverted by Cleopatra, Pompey can accomplish a decisive victory. To Pompey, young Caesar is not much more than a whelp, an upstart who has little support from the masses. As for Lepidus, Pompey simply discounts him as being no more than an ineffectual figurehead. This scene, then, gives us a view of the unstable political arena that such men as Pompey and Caesar move in. It is not a particularly attractive place. We also see how the struggles between Antony and Caesar are viewed by an outsider, a somewhat more objective viewer than either of the two triumvirs themselves. Unlike Caesar, though, Pompey does not underestimate Antony's ability. However, like Caesar, Pompey feels that Antony has gone to extremes in his total absorption in sensual pleasure to the exclusion of the real world. But if Antony has been lured so completely by love that he has forgotten his place as ruler of one-third of the empire, then perhaps he may be discounted, after all, as an enemy worth worrying about. At this point, Pompey seems fairly confident that he could win a war against the other two-thirds of the world – against Caesar and Lepidus – and thus place himself in a position to rule all of the empire.

ACT II – SCENE 2

Summary

At the beginning of the scene, in Rome, Lepidus meets briefly with Antony's friend Enobarbus. He asks Enobarbus to suggest to Antony that he exercise some tact and gentleness when he meets with Caesar. But Enobarbus, who is aware that Antony will not accept any suggestion that would make him appear weak to his rival, retorts that Antony will answer Caesar's questions in a manner worthy of himself. Antony will not demean himself to Caesar; if necessary, he will "speak as loud as Mars."

Caesar and Antony and their attendants enter, and Lepidus urges them to reaffirm their alliance before the security of the empire is destroyed. To emphasize the gravity of the situation, he uses the image of a surgeon who kills his patient by treating him too roughly; he hopes that this metaphor will vividly reveal what might happen to Rome if the two men don't mend their differences. He further compares the petty quarrels of Caesar and Antony to a minor wound; it would be a pity, he says, to lose the patient as a result.

The two rivals greet each other politely and proceed to discuss their problems. Antony asks Caesar directly if his (Antony's) living in Egypt has bothered Caesar. Caesar hesitates; he denies that he cares where Antony lives, unless Antony's purpose in living far from Rome was to "practice on my state" – that is, to plot against Caesar. This is a far different statement that Caesar makes in Antony's presence, compared to the bold words he used earlier when he was damning Antony's actions to Lepidus.

At this point, Antony asks Caesar what he meant when he used the word "practice." Caesar replies that he was referring to the attack made on him by Fulvia and Lucius Antony. Antony denies that he himself had any part in that plot, and he accuses Caesar of attempting to find a ground for a quarrel where none exists.

Having gotten nowhere with his arguments, Caesar says that he felt personally slighted when Antony refused to receive his ambassadors, an incident that we ourselves witnessed in the opening scene of the play. Since this accusation is true, Antony doesn't dispute it. On the contrary, he attempts to be conciliatory, without conceding any more than he has to.

Maecenas, an officer of Caesar's, suggests a change of subject, and Enobarbus adds that they should save their petty disagreements for a time when Pompey is no longer a threat. Antony tells Enobarbus to "speak no more." Since Enobarbus is only a soldier and not a statesman, he should not attempt to give advice to his superiors. Enobarbus responds by saying that he had forgotten that "truth should be silent," and that out of consideration for Antony he will be a "considerate stone," or, more colloquially, as "dumb as a stone."

Now that the generals' differences have been aired, Agrippa, a friend of Caesar's, suggests that their differences could be healed by a marriage that would cement their alliance, a marriage that would stand as a pledge of loyalty between them. He proposes that a marriage should be arranged between Antony (now a widower and, therefore, free to marry) and Caesar's sister, Octavia. Such a marriage would show the world the solidarity of the Triumvirate and would increase public confidence in their rule. Caesar watches to see how Antony reacts to the idea, and when he sees that Antony agrees to it immediately, he too gives his approval. Thus the two men shake hands to seal the agreement.

The discussion then turns to the subject of their common enemy, Pompey. Pompey's main strength is derived from his sea power because of his great naval fleet. At last, Antony is fully aware of the imminence of Pompey's threat, and he urges them all to make plans to face Pompey as soon as possible and defeat him before his power increases even more.

With their differences settled for the time being, the three triumvirs exit, leaving behind their officers, Enobarbus, Maecenas, and Agrippa. At this point, Enobarbus tells the others about Egypt, describing the luxury in which he and Antony lived. He describes Cleopatra, recalling one incident in particular, when she was sailing on the Nile in an elegant barge. From this description, it is possible to see how Antony could be so entranced by Cleopatra.

Enobarbus also describes one of the first times that the lovers met. Antony had invited Cleopatra to dine with him, but she insisted that she provide a dinner for him. Of course, he accepted. Comparing this meal to a dinner bought in a tavern, Enobarbus comments, without exaggeration, that Antony paid the bill with his heart.

Maecenas comments that it will be a sad thing indeed if Antony must now give up Cleopatra, since he is about to marry Octavia, but Enobarbus replies that Antony will *never* be able to leave Cleopatra, for no other woman can match her charm and beauty. Maecenas is not so sure; he says that if any woman can compare with Cleopatra, the beautiful and equally charming Octavia can. The scene ends with Enobarbus's accepting Agrippa's invitation to stay at his house while he and Antony are in Rome.

Commentary

This scene focuses on power, its psychology and its strategies. The language concerns politics and negotiation, with the key emphasis here on vantage status. Shakespeare's description of the dispute between the triumvirs as being similar to "murder [committed] in healing wounds" reflects the playwright's concern with the way in which nations are governed, and also the wit with which he can draw back and describe the situation so that we can see the dangers and the emotions involved.

The bickering in this scene, coupled with the astronomical illusions of the preceding scene with Pompey, suggest the precariousness of men's fortunes and the extent to which they are guided, often wrongly, by a lust for power.

Lepidus acts as a go-between to some extent—that is, he hopes that this meeting will enable Antony and Caesar to resolve their differences. Realistically, of course, he fears that the pride and the quick tempers of both men might interfere with any lasting reconciliation. In particular, he knows that Antony can only manipulate with great tact, and he does not think that the young Caesar, who at the moment feels as if he has been slighted, realizes this.

Although both generals pride themselves on their skill at high-level political negotiating, their egos, rather than their reason, appear to dominate this debate. The audience is left with an impression of totally useless and petty bickering. Caesar is obviously a testy and suspicious young man; he trusts no one, and while this is not an endearing quality, it will ultimately help him succeed in the world of politics and in his struggle for power.

This proposed marriage between Octavia and Antony involves yet another sharp difference in the two worlds of love and politics: in the scenes set in Egypt, we clearly saw that Antony and Cleopatra were genuinely attracted to each other. However, this Roman marriage between Octavia and Antony is a purely political alliance. Antony and Octavia hardly know each other. Love has no part in this union and, here, Shakespeare is emphasizing the political views of the powerful, practical Romans. This was no imaginative plot complication; power is a strong aphrodisiac.

ACT II – SCENE 3

Summary

As the scene opens, still in Rome, Antony and Octavia, the betrothed couple, bid each other good night, and Antony admonishes Octavia not to believe all that she hears of him. Seemingly, he hopes to reassure his future wife that he will be a good husband, in spite of his past reputation for sexual excesses. His words, however, ring hollow at this point.

As Octavia and her brother Caesar leave, the soothsayer from Egypt enters, and Antony is reminded of Egypt and all his pleasures there. Antony asks the soothsayer, "Whose fortunes shall rise higher, Caesar's or mine?" The soothsayer warns Antony that he can never achieve any great success so long as he remains "by [Caesar's] side," for Caesar will always overshadow him. This disturbs Antony, and he abruptly tells the Egyptian not to speak of such things. Instead, he turns his attention to tactical matters. He speaks of a plan to send his officer Ventidius to Parthia to suppress some trouble in the East.

Antony is troubled; he cannot forget what he has just been told by the soothsayer. He is also troubled by his memories of how he has always fared the worse in any competition with Caesar, even in mere games. He wonders if the soothsayer has indeed spoken truthfully. But again he resolves to put such matters out of his mind, and he decides impulsively to go to Egypt ("In the East my pleasure lies"). Although he will soon marry Octavia, he cannot forget his strong passion for Cleopatra, and although he tried to reassure Octavia that he would be a good husband, and despite the fact that he wants to maintain harmony between himself and Caesar, Antony decides that he must go to Cleopatra. He is not an evil man; he does not purposely want to hurt Octavia, but he cannot calm his passions. Politics are one matter, but love is another, and thus we see his duplicity in the fact that he can pledge his loyalty to Octavia one minute, while planning all the while to return to his real love, Cleopatra, as soon as possible. While such marriages of convenience were no doubt common and quite acceptable, Antony's sudden shifts of thought, and especially his surges of desire, again illustrate how Antony is caught between the pressing duties of Rome and the urgent demands of love. In one moment, Antony seems to be all business — planning military strategy like a militaristic Roman general — and in the next minute, he can think of nothing but Cleopatra and the pleasure that awaits him in Egypt. Significantly, at this point, Antony cannot face the challenge of facing up to Caesar and testing his valor, so, for the moment, he puts all thoughts of that problem out of his mind and decides to hurry back to Cleopatra.

Commentary

This scene illustrates very briefly and very succinctly Antony's greatest weakness: his inability to face facts. He is not wholly honest with himself, and so he fares poorly when he is matched with those who are more self-confident than he is. Antony's weakest flaw of all, however, is his overpowering passion for Cleopatra — especially its illegitimacy. This fact was not lost on Shakespeare's audience; great love stories were often told and much admired, but the *ideal* love story centered on a love that was climaxed by marriage. Here, this is impossible; despite Antony's love for Cleopatra, it has led him to duplicity, and eventually it will cause his death. The question which Shakespeare is already posing for us is whether or not Antony's means of achieving his love's desires are justified.

ACT II — SCENE 4

Summary

As the scene opens in Rome, Lepidus is being escorted by two officers, Maecenas and Agrippa, and after they have walked with him awhile, he tells them that they may return to their business, which at this point is to prepare for possible battle with Pompey.

Commentary

This transition scene seems to serve no critical purpose, except to remind the audience of the counterforce to love in this drama — that is, the force of politics and power, twin forces which are forever struggling for Antony's loyalty. We are also reminded again that intrigue abounds, and that events will soon be beginning to move rapidly toward a crisis.

ACT II – SCENE 5

Summary

Cleopatra is bored and pensive as this scene opens in Alexandria. She turns to her servants and asks them to amuse her. She wants Charmian to play billiards with her, but Charmian begs off and suggests that Cleopatra play billiards instead with Mardian, the eunuch. The idea of thrusting balls into pockets with a long billiard stick gives Cleopatra plenty of opportunity to tease the eunuch about his physical disability; the many double entendres of the dialogue in this scene no doubt amused Shakespeare's audience and provided a short and rather bawdy comic interlude.

As Charmian and her mistress talk together, Cleopatra reminisces about the things which she and Antony did together; she recalls their going fishing together and how she tricked Antony into catching an old salt fish. She also tells about another time, when they pretended to be Hercules and Omphale, who enslaved Hercules with her charms and made him wear her clothes as a joke, while she strutted around wearing his sword.

A messenger enters then with news of Antony, and Cleopatra is so excited that she hardly gives him a chance to speak. She interrupts him, she rambles, she threatens him with punishment if the news is bad, and then she promises him wealth if the news is good. The messenger is understandably anxious. He rightly suspects that his queen will *not* be pleased to learn that Antony has made friends with Caesar and that he has married Octavia.

Upon hearing the news, Cleopatra strikes the messenger and threatens to stab him. She later regrets her impulsiveness, however, for she realizes that it is ignoble for one in power to hit someone who has done no wrong and who is powerless to defend himself. She asks that the messenger be brought back to her, and she asks him to tell her more about what has happened. Again she hears the incredible news, and again she orders the messenger from her sight. Cleopatra is grief-stricken; she can think of nothing but her need to get away and hide. She wants to be alone with her distress, but she wants to know more. Since the messenger is too frightened to speak further in her presence, she sends her servant Alexas after him. She wants Alexas to find out what he can and to report back to her what Octavia is like. Although Cleopatra is deeply hurt, she has not been defeated yet. If she can find out what kind of woman Octavia is, she can make plans to win Antony back.

Commentary

This scene illustrates yet another facet of the complex personality of Cleopatra. Although at times she can be giddy and superficial, the depth of her feeling for Antony is not shallow. In this scene, for example, we also see evidence of her emotional fury. The cause is clear: the most terrible thing she could imagine in her relationship with Antony has happened: Antony is involved with another woman, and not only is he involved with her, but he has *married* her. Yet Cleopatra recovers sufficiently to take some tentative steps to find out if she can regain Antony's love. This in itself is proof of her inner strength and resourcefulness.

Cleopatra is a person of extremes—that is, she is dramatic and emotional, to excess, but she is also a warm and vulnerable woman, and she is mature enough to be rightly suspicious of Antony. In fact, her passion for Antony frightens her; we see evidence of this when she realizes that she was wrong when she blamed the messenger for telling her that Antony had married Octavia. Even though she is an absolute ruler, she does not have the right to punish a messenger by threatening him with a knife for the content of a distressing message.

ACT II – SCENE 6

Summary

The focus of this scene, set near Misenum, centers on the meeting of Caesar, Antony, Lepidus, and Pompey: earlier, the triumvirs sent a letter to Pompey: in it, they said that they were prepared to allow Pompey to rule Sicily and Sardinia if he would agree to "rid all the sea of pirates" and send an annual tribute of wheat to Rome. Pompey is prepared to accept the offer, but he says that Mark Antony has put him to "some impatience." Pompey reminds Antony of past debts; for example, Lucius, Antony's brother, and Fulvia, Antony's late wife, joined with Caesar and attacked Pompey. Antony acknowledges this fact. Antony and Pompey then exchange pleasantries about the good life in the East, while Caesar remains silent; negotiations are concluded for the time being. Pompey then invites them all to celebrate the treaty by dining aboard his galley.

Pompey comments on the fine cuisine of Egypt, and he also mentions how (Julius) Caesar enjoyed life there, relating how "a certain queen" was smuggled in to Caesar. He presses for more details, and Enobarbus explains that the queen was carried secretly to Caesar "in a mattress." Pompey suddenly recognizes Enobarbus; he remembers him as being a good soldier. Honest as always, Enobarbus returns the greeting by admitting that although he has never much cared for Pompey, he has always admired Pompey's skill and ability as a general.

All exit then, except Enobarbus and Pompey's officer, the pirate Menas. The two men discuss the treaty that has just been made. Menas claims that Pompey placated too easily; Pompey's father, Pompey the Great, would never have settled on terms so favorable to the Romans. Enobarbus agrees; he says that Pompey may have seriously reduced his chance of becoming a powerful force in the empire. Menas then asks why Antony has come to Rome; it was thought by many, he says, that Antony had married Cleopatra and ruled in Egypt. Enobarbus tells him, however, that Antony is now married to Octavia, an arrangement which they both realize was a political match. Enobarbus cynically predicts that Antony will betray Octavia by returning to Cleopatra. Caesar, they know, will be enraged.

Commentary

At this point, it seems as if the threat to the Triumvirate from without—that is, from Pompey—will be defused, and the struggle will again focus on the real issue at stake: the conflict between Caesar and Antony.

ACT II – SCENE 7

Summary

As the scene opens on Pompey's galley, the servants are getting ready for the feast; and they gossip among themselves, joking that the three Romans are already well on the way to becoming drunk. They have been taking turns pouring part of their wine into Lepidus's glass, and he is getting even more intoxicated than the others, and he doesn't even realize that they are amusing themselves with jokes at his expense.

Caesar and Antony lose no opportunity to taunt each other, a situation which the drunken Lepidus ineptly tries to reconcile. Here again, the servants comment shrewdly that it is a sorry fact that although Lepidus is one of the triumvirs (and theoretically one of the most powerful men in the world), he is really only a figurehead. The other two triumvirs have no respect for his opinions nor for his ability as a leader; rather, they see his role as no more than that of a bit player in a major drama; he balances their power, and he serves as a buffer to prevent the worst effects of their rivalry.

Commentary

Act II ends on a rather light note, but once again the theme of excess is repeated. It might also be noted that excess and indulgence are not inherent vices of the Egyptians, as the Romans would like to think. They are states of mind, attitudes, and choices that can exist anywhere, as the party aboard Pompey's barge illustrates.

ACT III – SCENE 1

Summary

The act opens on a plain in Syria. Ventidius, a Roman officer, was sent to fight the Parthians by Antony at the end of Act II, Scene 3. It is not clear how much time has passed, but in this scene, Ventidius has returned to Rome, and he describes his victory over the Parthians to Silius, one of his officers. Ventidius relates how he killed Pacorus, the Parthian king's son in revenge for the death of

Marcus Crassus, a noble Roman, killed by the Parthians in another battle in which Crassus's entire force was annihilated. Silius encourages Ventidius to make the most of his victory by returning home in triumph, but Ventidius refuses, noting that it is better not to appear too successful, lest he shame his commander, Antony, by comparison. He tells about another officer of Antony's, Sossius, who served well in Syria, but fell out of favor; it is implied that his great success as a warrior may have had something to do with it.

Silius praises Ventidius's discretion, and Ventidius says that he will write to tell Antony about the victory, although he will be careful not to boast.

Commentary

The subject matter of the entirety of Act III is war, and this chapter serves to introduce this facet of the play to the audience while also continuing the theme of the on-going foreign battles, a theme that has been woven into the plot by events in earlier scenes, such as Antony's command to Ventidius in Act II.

This scene focuses primarily on the relationship between war and power. Not only are the rival generals, Caesar and Antony, vying against each other for ultimate power, but the lesser officers are also continually seeking their own advancement. Ventidius is wise here to avoid seeking excessive military glory. He does not want Antony to think he is trying to rival him in military achievements.

The language used by Shakespeare in this brief scene suggests the power, the action, and the cruelty of war. The Parthians, a fierce nation of horsemen, are described as being "darting" Parthians. It has been suggested by several critics that this word was meant to refer to the Parthian practice of turning around to shoot arrows at their enemy while riding away from them. Whatever their military strategy, however, they have been defeated.

Perhaps it should be noted that Shakespeare was paralleling history when he made Ventidius cautious about boasting too much of his success. Ventidius is wary of Antony's thinking that he might perhaps be trying to become "his captain's captain"; a soldier should not be so successful that he overshadows his commander. This concern with ambition and the consequences of seeming too ambitious are understandable when we consider the means used at that time to acquire power. Soldier-emperors like Antony or Caesar would inevitably be suspicious of any officer who might remind them too much of themselves during their earlier careers when they were filled with bravery and unbridled ambition.

Silius praises Ventidius for having that "distinction" (discretion) without which a skilled soldier grants no "distinction" (honor) at all. This play on words suggests the dual qualities which are the key ingredients for the best officers: valor and the discretion to know when to act and when not to.

There is some irony in the contrast between the cautious and soldierly Ventidius and the more impulsive Antony. As we shall see later in this act, Antony actually *lacks* that very discretion talked about here when he plans his battles. Tragically, it leads to his own destruction.

ACT III – SCENE 2

Summary

As this scene opens, in Rome, Agrippa and Enobarbus enter and discuss recent events. Octavia is to leave Rome with her new husband, Antony. Caesar is sad to see her go, and, for the moment, Lepidus is the butt of everyone's joking. For example, they discuss Lepidus's excessive devotion to both Caesar *and* Antony and his futile attempts to act as a mediator between them. This is a fittingly ironic foreshadowing of what is soon to happen, for Caesar, Antony, Lepidus, and Octavia enter, and they begin to discuss Octavia's imminent departure with Antony. Like Lepidus, she too is a mediator who loves both her brother and her husband, but she senses a conflict that she feels is somehow tragic.

Caesar admonishes Antony to take good care of his sister, and Antony says he must not seek fault where none exists. He promises that Caesar will find no "cause . . . for what [he seems] to fear"; Antony will be kind to Octavia. Enobarbus and Agrippa, meanwhile, make asides concerning Caesar, comparing his appearance to that of an ill-tempered horse. They wonder if Caesar will cry (he is apparently trying not to), yet even Antony has wept before, they note, and he is certainly no less masculine for having done so. The two men make their farewells, and Antony and Caesar embrace briefly.

Commentary

The gossipy tone in the first part of the scene, where Agrippa and Enobarbus make fun of the futile efforts of Lepidus to be loyal to both Antony and Caesar, foreshadows the fact that Octavia's role as a mediator will also prove ultimately unsuccessful. Yet, for now, the key focus is on Lepidus; he is described by Enobarbus as suffering from the "green-sickness" ever since Pompey's feast, described earlier. "Green-sickness" was an ailment supposedly suffered by adolescent girls when they fell in love; they became wan and weak from worry about their lovers. In this context, it probably refers to the painful hangover that Lepidus probably suffered the day after he was encouraged to drink too much at the banquet.

Lepidus is said to love both Caesar and Antony, and to be totally devoted to both men. Of course, this is impossible. The two men are rivals. Yet it is true that Lepidus is very much like a young girl — that is, he is unable to decide to whom he should give his loyalty. And in comparison to both Antony and Caesar, Lepidus has so little power that all he can do is fret and worry. Agrippa says bluntly, "both he loves," to which Enobarbus retorts, "They are his shards, and he their beetle." This figure of speech refers to the shiny wing-cases of beetles which were called "shards" because of their resemblance to fragments of shiny pottery or glass. Figuratively, Lepidus is like a beetle in that he is helpless without his bright wings — Antony and Caesar. In addition, Lepidus can be compared to the dull-colored insect whose bright wings are *far* more noticeable than the small little body to which the wings are attached.

Agrippa and Enobarbus leave then, as the others enter, and Caesar tells Antony:

> Let not the piece of virtue which is set
> Betwixt us as the cement of our love,
> To keep it builded, be the ram to batter
> The fortress of it; for better might we
> Have loved without this mean, if on both parts
> This be not cherish'd
>
> (29-34)

The image here that Caesar evokes is of a building, and the love of the two men for the virtuous Octavia is the cement. (She is the

"piece" or masterpiece of virtue referred to here). But were Octavia
to be ill-treated, or if she were to be considered as a hostage, she
would be the battering ram that would cause the whole structure of
their precarious alliance to crumble. Thus, Caesar says that he
would hate Antony more if Octavia were to be misused than he
would hate Antony if Octavia had never been given to him to "cement" their peace.

Antony warns Caesar not to pursue this mistrust any further,
lest he (Antony) take offense at it. Caesar then says goodbye to Octavia, who is weeping; her tears, Antony gallantly describes as being
like "April's [showers] in her eyes; it is love's spring." He suggests
that like the spring rains that water the ground, her tears com-
memorate the beginning of the growth of their love for one another.

When Octavia says that she wishes to whisper in Caesar's ear,
perhaps to give some private message or ask that he not forget her,
he is touched by her grief. Antony too is affected, and again he tries
to be gallant. He suggests that she is too filled with emotion to
speak clearly, and like "the swan's down-feather/ That stands upon
the swell at full of tide," she cannot clearly express her loyalty and
love to either Caesar or Antony—that she is torn by her devotion to
both, and thus she turns first one way and then another, like a
feather fluttering on the water. This image aptly sums up her help-
lessness as an object who will be used later by both men in their
competing for power.

Enobarbus and Agrippa observe Caesar and Antony, and they
comment that Caesar "has a cloud in his face," meaning that he is
either frowning or attempting to suppress tears. Agrippa notes that
Antony, in contrast, was not too proud to weep when Julius Caesar
was killed, nor later when Brutus was slain; in neither case was he
considered less manly for having wept. Enobarbus quips that Antony did indeed have a lot of "rheumy colds" that year, meaning that
he wept a lot, and he suggests that Antony perhaps wept because of
what he had destroyed—meaning Brutus.

The soldiers' comments are not very complimentary to either of
the triumvirs. It is hinted that Caesar refrains from crying because
he is too insecure to permit himself to show any weakness, while Antony almost too willingly expresses emotions that perhaps he
doesn't actually feel. Thus, his gallantry towards Octavia may rest
on a questionable basis—that is, his devotion to her is likely to be
short-lived.

ACT III – SCENE 3

Summary

This scene returns us to Alexandria and provides us with some light comic relief as Cleopatra questions a messenger about Octavia. This is the same messenger whom she terrorized earlier when he told her about Antony's marriage. Now she is pleasant and ingratiating as she tries to find out what her new rival is like. After she questions the messenger about Octavia's manner and appearance, she is satisfied with the answers he gives her, and she pays him well for the good news.

Commentary

Because of Cleopatra's earlier fury, it is quite understandable that this messenger would be wary of arousing the queen's ire. He is very careful to describe Octavia in such vague and neutral terms that Cleopatra can infer what she likes from them. And this she does: Cleopatra wants to be reassured, and so she interprets the messenger's words to suit herself. He says that Octavia is not tall; accordingly, Cleopatra assumes that Octavia is dwarfish, or dumpy. The messenger says that Octavia is "low-voiced," and Cleopatra interprets this as meaning that she is "dull of tongue." She then asks the messenger if there is "majesty in her gait," and he replies, "She creeps." Cleopatra is pleased by this description, and she compliments his "good judgment."

ACT III – SCENE 4

Summary

The scene opens in Athens, in the middle of a conversation between Antony and Octavia. Apparently they have been discussing the recent activities of Caesar, and Octavia defends Caesar; she urges Antony not to take offense at what Caesar might have said about him. Caesar is preparing for war, and Antony tells Octavia that he too must prepare, and that his preparations will overshadow those of her brother. He encourages his wife to return to Rome, presumably to act as a mediator and reduce the growing hostility between Caesar and Antony.

Commentary

This brief scene highlights the fact that Octavia is trying to be a peacemaker between her brother and Antony. She will not succeed, and the urgency with which Antony insists that she should go to Rome makes one question his motives. It is almost certain that he is anxious to rendezvous in Alexandria with Cleopatra.

ACT III – SCENE 5

Summary

While Antony and Octavia, in Athens, discuss matters in one part of the house, Enobarbus and Eros (a friend of Antony) talk about recent events. Eros tells Enobarbus that as soon as Caesar and Lepidus defeated Pompey, Caesar turned on Lepidus and accused him of treachery. Lepidus now awaits death in a prison cell.

Enobarbus asks where Antony is, and Eros replies that he is in the garden and that he is angry about what has happened. Antony cries out in vain that Lepidus was a fool for submitting to Caesar; in addition, he mutters threats to kill the officer who murdered Pompey. At this point, Enobarbus is summoned by Antony, and the two men exit.

Commentary

Basically, this scene gives us an important piece of information about Lepidus, and, equally important, it shows us Antony's reaction to Lepidus's imprisonment. We are almost certain that the recent bond between Antony and Caesar has begun to crack. Clearly, Antony will not allow himself to be manipulated as easily by Caesar as Lepidus was. In addition, it seems as if Caesar is rapidly trying to consolidate his power. The outcome of the rivalry between these two fiery, ambitious triumvirs will ultimately depend on whether or not Antony can counter Caesar's strategies. It seems unlikely that he can; as we shall see, he does not. The singleness of purpose that is characteristic of Caesar (to the point of being a fault) is not a trait that Antony shares. Torn by his desire to spend his time with Cleopatra and his equally potent desire for power in Rome, Antony unfortunately hesitates too frequently and too long about what he will do.

The two lieutenants comment that Caesar and Antony are a couple of "chaps" (a pun meaning "fellows" and also "jaws") who will grind up men like food, themselves included. The truth of this observation will soon be revealed as Caesar, Antony, and Cleopatra become increasingly embroiled in their individual wars and intrigues.

ACT III – SCENE 6

Summary

The scene opens in Rome. Antony has now returned to Egypt, and Caesar tells two of his officers, Maecenas and Agrippa, about Antony's recent activities there. Antony has formally appointed Cleopatra to be Queen of Egypt, lower Syria, Cyprus, and Lydia, and he has also made his two small sons titular kings of various lands which he has conquered. Caesar interprets Antony's actions as being political ploys to usurp the authority of Rome; thus, they are an insult to both the empire and to Caesar personally.

As a further insult to himself, Caesar says, Antony (in a letter, apparently) has accused Caesar of not giving him his due portion of Pompey's realm in Sicily and that he has also suggested that Caesar's detention of Lepidus was solely for the purpose of acquiring his property. Caesar says that he has sent a messenger to explain why Lepidus was arrested. He also agrees to grant Antony part of the kingdom that he, Caesar, has conquered, but only if Antony reciprocates by granting him land from his own conquests. He suspects, however, that Antony will never agree to this.

Octavia arrives with her attendants, and Caesar chides her for giving him no warning that she was coming; he had no time to welcome her with proper ceremony. She tells him that she heard that Caesar was making preparations for war, and when she begged to return, Antony allowed her to do so.

Caesar tells his sister that Antony's real reason for permitting her to return to Rome was for one reason only: so that Antony could return to Cleopatra. Octavia is agonized that her brother, Caesar, and her new husband, Antony, "do afflict each other."

Commentary

Here we see Caeser finally deciding to take overt action against Antony. He would not have dared to do so earlier, but because of Antony's return to Egypt, because of Antony's assertion of military and political authority there, and because of Antony's adulterous insults to Octavia, Caesar now has sufficient reasons to do what he has wanted to do all the time – that is, he can now attack Antony, defeat him, and become sole ruler of the world.

If Antony were more farsighted and if he had realized what an ambitious foe Caesar was, perhaps he would have been more careful in giving Caesar an excuse to attack him. But one suspects that even if Antony had not given Caesar sufficient reasons to provoke him, Caesar would have created them. Very simply, Caesar is overly ambitious and pathologically power-hungry.

When we hear Caesar say that he explained to Antony in a letter that Lepidus was deposed because he was "too cruel;/ That he his high authority abus'd," one should not miss the irony here. Of all people, the ineffectual and powerless Lepidus is most unlikely to have abused his authority. It is Caesar *himself* who would be most likely to abuse "high authority." But such duplicity is as typical of Caesar in achieving his goals as it is of Antony and Cleopatra. Caesar deceives himself; he rationalizes acts that further his ambition, and Antony likewise deceives himself when he believes that what he is doing will have no consequences; naively, Antony sees no danger in spending time with Cleopatra. As another example of self-deception, we have just witnessed how Cleopatra deceives herself; she interpreted the messenger's description of Octavia as being wholly negative in order to satisfy her need to believe that it is she alone whom Antony really cares for.

Caesar's duplicity here is evident even in the way he scolds Octavia for not giving him a chance to welcome her properly. In fact, he is really less concerned about *her* than he is about his last opportunity to show the world how badly Antony has treated his sister. This motive is unstated, but it is clearly consistent with the self-serving way in which he has explained other events – for example, Lepidus's fall from favor.

Summary

Shakespeare next focuses on several battle scenes. The first opens at Antony's camp, where Antony, Cleopatra, and Enobarbus are planning their strategy. The main issue concerns whether or not they will fight Caesar on land or on sea. Against his better judgment, Antony chooses to fight Caesar on the sea.

Commentary

As the scene opens, Enobarbus bitterly chides Cleopatra for being present on the battlefield. She retorts that since Rome has declared war on her and Antony, she has the right to be present.

Antony and Canidius enter, and Antony reports on Caesar's past victories at sea. Cleopatra chides her lover for not taking swifter action against Caesar, and Antony agrees: if Caesar chooses to fight "by the sea," Antony will do likewise; Antony's valor is at stake. Caesar "dares us to it," he says. Enobarbus objects that this is poor planning, that Antony's forces are not as well-equipped to take to the sea as Caesar's are. Caesar's men, he says, are experienced, and his ships are light and swift. By comparison, Antony's forces have been hastily drawn together, and many of them are inexperienced in battle. But Antony impulsively insists on a sea battle. He will not retreat from Caesar's challenge.

Enobarbus, Antony's loyal advisor and friend, again patiently tries to explain that if Antony pursues this course of action he will "throw away the absolute soldiership [he has] by land." But Antony replies again, "I'll fight at sea." The length and patience of Enobarbus's speeches and the repetition and brevity of Antony's replies all illustrate Antony's impulsiveness. He doesn't offer a reason why he feels that a battle on the sea is a good choice; he simply insists upon it. At this point, Cleopatra offers him the use of sixty ships, and he accepts.

A soldier enters and begs Antony not to fight Caesar at sea. But Antony rejects this advice. Antony, Cleopatra, and Enobarbus leave then, and the unnamed soldier and Canidius remain. The two men blame Antony's foolish and headstrong decisions on Cleopatra's influence. There is, of course, reason enough to accept their evaluation of the situation, but we should be careful to assess these characters' opinions. Shakespeare does not allow any single character in this play to speak as an all-knowing mouthpiece. Rather, he gives us a variety of viewpoints and lets the audience discern where the truth of the drama lies and what the decisive motivations are for the action.

ACT III – SCENE 8

Summary

This brief scene reveals the exchange between Caesar and his trusted lieutenant Taurus and establishes the fact that Caesar's army will indeed attack by sea, and that Caesar believes that this move will prove advantageous to his side: "Our fortune lies upon this jump," he boasts.

Commentary

After Shakespeare has focused on Antony for several scenes, he now turns his attention to Caesar. Confident and proud, Caesar is convinced that victory awaits him.

ACT III – SCENE 9

Summary

Antony and Enobarbus meet in an equally brief scene and plan to position their men so that they can see how many ships Caesar has sent and act accordingly.

Commentary

It seems as though Antony is planning a defensive campaign because he decides to leave part of the land forces under Enobarbus's command.

ACT III – SCENE 10

Summary

Canidius with his armies and Taurus with his troops are seen briefly on the stage. They exit, and the audience hears offstage the noise of the battle at sea. Enobarbus and Scarus, another soldier, enter, and we learn that Antony's fleet has retreated. Scarus exclaims that because of Antony's ignorance they have lost their chance to be rulers of a segment (a cantle) of the empire. Scarus, in describing the battle, blames the defeat on the presence of Cleopatra. She retreated first ("like a cow in June"), and Antony followed her rather than staying to fight.

Canidius says that Antony has not lived up to his reputation; Canidius has decided to surrender to Caesar. While Enobarbus agrees with Canidius that Caesar will undoubtedly win, he vows to stay on with Antony, although the decision is against his better judgment.

ACT III – SCENE 11

Summary

Instead of staying to battle Caesar's forces, Antony is defeated in battle when he follows Cleopatra's sudden retreat. He is despondent and is not comforted even when Cleopatra enters and tries to soothe him. On the contrary, he is so ashamed of his cowardice that to some extent he places the blame upon her. Cleopatra apologizes, but there is, in fact, nothing to apologize for; obviously, Antony cares for her above all else. For this, no apology is possible. He changes the subject and tells her that he has sent Euphronius, their children's tutor, as an ambassador to request the terms of a peace treaty.

Commentary

In one sense, Antony is at his weakest and most pitiful in this scene. He is utterly defeated because of his own poor judgment (or perhaps his cowardice), and yet he cannot resist making excuses; in particular, he thinks that it is possible that he was so bewitched by "Egypt" that his judgment was affected. Yet at the same time, he is aware that this is only partly true: his defeat was also the result of his own choice – that is, he placed Cleopatra above all else in his life. And in the end, he says he is not sorry that he made this choice. Of course, ideally, he would have liked to have won the battle and spent as much time as possible with Cleopatra, but he failed. He tried, however, and one can easily suspect that a part of Antony's shame

comes from the knowledge that he was defeated by a young upstart
for whom he had little respect. Underestimating Caesar was an error
that he, an experienced soldier, should have foreseen and avoided.

Antony's unfortunately underrated estimate of his enemy
focuses, at times, on imaginative fantasy. Caesar, he says, behaved
in battle unlike a soldier. He says that Caesar held his sword "like a
dancer," meaning that he wore it more as an ornament than used it
as a warrior. Still rationalizing, Antony also accuses Caesar of having depended on his lieutenants rather than getting involved in the
actual fighting himself. These are scenes of frustration, confusion,
and self-pity. Antony prided himself in being a rational general. His
love for Cleopatra has changed that, and in the next few scenes, at
times he will seem to be petty, over-critical, and often too eager to
make excuses for himself. That this is probably the result of his
defeat and not a part of his normal personality is shown by Iras's
comment that Antony is "unqualitied with very shame"—that is, he
is not acting like himself because of the great shame that he suffers.

ACT III – SCENE 12

Summary

In his camp in Egypt, Caesar is meeting with some of his officers and also with Antony's ambassador, Euphronius. Euphronius
presents Antony's requests to Caesar: Antony requests to be allowed to remain in Egypt, but if that is impossible, he asks that he
at least be allowed to live as a private citizen in Athens. Euphronius
also tells Caesar that Cleopatra acknowledges that Caesar is the victor and the supreme ruler of them all, but she requests that she be
permitted to remain as Queen of Egypt and to retain the crown of
the Ptolemies, the Egyptian royal family, for her heirs.

Caesar ignores Antony's request and makes an offer to Cleopatra: if she will betray Antony and drive him from Egypt, or kill
him there, then he might consider her requests. Caesar then orders
his servant Thyreus to return to Cleopatra with Caesar's answer. He
comments that women are no stronger than their own interests, and
that, being a woman, Cleopatra can probably be bribed with the
promise of her own safety in exchange for Antony's life.

Commentary

Casear's own insecurity is revealed here by the harshness of his settlement. Certainly he has the right to demand Antony's life, but most Romans were known for being relatively generous to those whom they conquered. In this case, however, Caesar may be a more accurate judge of Antony's character than Antony was of Caesar's. Caesar knows, and rightly so, that he can never really feel safe as long as Antony is alive or free. Note, however, that Caesar is a very poor judge of Cleopatra's character. Since he can't see beyond the popular stereotype of her as being little more than a prostitute, he believes that she can easily be bought. This is not an unusual mistake for someone like Caesar to make; as far as we know, he does not really know what it is like to fall in love. Here, Caesar shows himself to be the complete soldier or strategist, not only in his ignorance about aspects of life not connected with war or politics, but also in the care he takes in his negotiations. He instructs Thyreus to be "cunning." Interestingly, Caesar is at *his* most "cunning" here, for he makes no firm promises to do anything at all for Cleopatra.

ACT III – SCENE 13

Summary

In Alexandria, Cleopatra and her servants (including Antony's cynical officer Enobarbus) discuss their plight. Cleopatra asks Enobarbus if the defeat was truly Antony's fault or if it was the fault of the Egyptians. Enobarbus answers that Antony was solely at fault, but not only for his retreat. He also erred when he made "his will [the] Lord of his reason." Enobarbus adds that Antony's love and/or lust for Cleopatra affected his judgment; this, in his soldier's opinion, " 'Twas a shame no less/ Than was his loss."

At this point, Antony and Euphronius enter. Apparently, Euphronius has told Antony what Caesar said, and Antony instructs Euphronius to relate the news to Cleopatra so that she may decide what action she wishes to take. Antony then scornfully tells her that the "boy Caesar" wishes her to send "this grizzled head" (Antony's) to him in exchange for her freedom. He is insulted by Caesar's treatment, and he is piqued that the "boy" general would flatter or attempt to persuade Cleopatra in such a way. Antony tells Cleopatra that he dares Caesar to meet him in a one-to-one match ("ourselves alone"). He is confident that he, Antony, will prove to be the victor.

Antony and Euphronius leave, and Enobarbus remarks to himself that it is possible that Caesar might agree to such a match, but in his opinion, it would be foolish. He believes that Antony's judgment is "a parcel of [his] fortunes," and that his bad luck is reflected in his bad judgment.

A servant enters to tell Cleopatra that a messenger from Caesar has arrived. The queen is offended by the brusqueness of his entrance, and Enobarbus again comments cynically on their fate, yet finally he concludes that there *is* a certain amount of honor even in following a fallen lord.

The messenger is Thyreus, and he states to Cleopatra that he would like to speak with her privately. She says, however, that there are only friends present; they all may hear what he has to say. Thyreus begins and attempts to gain Cleopatra's confidence, while actually promising nothing. He urges her to trust Caesar and insinuates that it is well known that she did not stay with Antony freely, but rather because she was forced to, perhaps to placate him in order to protect her realm.

Cleopatra appears to agree with what Thyreus says, and thus Enobarbus stalks off, convinced that all of Antony's friends, even Cleopatra, are now deserting him. She concedes that Caesar *is* the victor, then says little else except to acknowledge that single fact. Thyreus kneels to kiss her hand in reply just as Antony and Enobarbus enter. The gesture is courteous, but could not have been timed worse. Antony enters, and he is outraged. He orders Thyreus to be punished for his impertinence, and then he turns on Cleopatra and rages at her faithlessness. He is quite explicit about her faults, using words similar to those which she used against him when she accused him of faithlessness in the past. The servants reenter with the beaten Thyreus, and Antony sends him back to Caesar, telling him to tell his general that if he doesn't like the treatment that the messenger received from Antony, then he can do as he likes with *his* hostage (Hipparchus, who, according to Plutarch, hoped to save his life and apparently deserted Antony and joined Caesar).

When Antony returns, he begins to berate Cleopatra again, and she asks him, "Not know me yet?" This stops him, and she affirms that it is he whom she loves and no one else; all else was a charade. Antony, as quickly as he was enraged, is apparently satisfied with her explanation, and they are reconciled. He vows to fight Caesar to the end. Then, as Antony and Cleopatra leave to spend her birthday night together, he brags that not even death itself will frighten him in what will probably be the final battle; he will "contend even with [Death's] pestilent scythe."

Only Enobarbus is left on stage, and he continues to comment on Antony's loss of judgment. More valor, he suggests, will not compensate now: "When valor preys on reason, it eats the sword it fights with." Utterly disgusted and disappointed in his doomed master, the once loyal Enobarbus finally decides that he must desert Antony if it is possible to do so.

Commentary

Cleopatra's character begins to reveal a more complex nature than we have heretofore seen. Although her methods are devious, her purpose in this scene seems more mature and noble, in the sense that she never wavers from her loyalty to Antony. Likewise, Antony appears brave and generous. But, as always, he is also impulsive and stubborn. He rapidly jumps to the conclusion that Cleopatra is altering her loyalties, when in fact she is not. Yet even Enobarbus thinks that Cleopatra may be making a truce with Thyreus. Throughout the play we see that the men generally give Cleopatra less credit than she deserves, and we shall see that even Antony, though temporarily reassured, will doubt her again.

ACT IV – SCENE 1

Summary

At Caesar's camp outside Alexandria, Agrippa and Maecenas attend their general. He is reading an insulting letter from Antony, and after he finishes, he considers its contents. "He calls me boy," Caesar says, and he adds that Antony challenges him to "personal combat." Prudently, Caesar refuses to accept the challenge.

Maecenas advises Caesar to press forward in the battle while Antony is so obviously at a disadvantage. Caesar agrees, for not only is his army strong, but he has gained additional men who have deserted Antony's army.

Commentary

At this point, Shakespeare's vision of Caesar does not change; he will remain throughout the rest of the drama as a cool, calculating strategist. While Antony's defeat is a loss of honor to Antony, a matter to be resolved on the dueling field, to Caesar it is nothing more or less than the result of a battle. Caesar is irritated at Antony's slighting remarks, but unlike his foe, he does not let his emotions affect his judgment. There remains for him one single goal: total victory. In order to achieve this goal, he needs his army; wisely, he is not willing to gamble on his own prowess when he is convinced that his army can destroy Antony and his forces. It is far wiser strategy, he believes, to "laugh at [the] challenge . . . [of] the old ruffian."

ACT IV – SCENE 2

Summary

The scene now shifts to Cleopatra's palace and focuses on Antony's reaction to Caesar's refusal to fight in "personal combat." Antony is surprised at Caesar's refusal, but he vows that he will beat him in battle.

He then calls for a meal to be served, and he compliments his servants for their loyalty. He speaks as if this is the last night they will serve him, and before long they are all weeping; even the hardened old Enobarbus is "onion-eyed" and begs Antony not to give them such discomfort, and Antony responds by laughing. He did not mean to be taken seriously, he says, and he assures those present that he expects victory – not defeat.

Commentary

Antony reveals two interesting character traits here: bravado and sentimentality. At their best, these qualities give Antony great courage and a generous and forgiving nature, but at their worst they become sentimental pap, which Enobarbus is quick to point out.

ACT IV – SCENE 3

Summary

Antony's soldiers stand guard before Cleopatra's palace; all of them are aware that this is the night before the final battle that shall determine Antony's fate. Suddenly they hear strange noises and eerie music, and one soldier claims that this is an ill omen from the god Hercules, from whom Antony is believed to be descended. The soldier fears that these events are a sign that the god no longer favors Antony. The soldiers attempt to follow the source of the music but cannot discover it.

Commentary

Both classical and Elizabethan accounts of the Battle of Actium mention the occurrence of supernatural omens before the battle. Plutarch's version of these events varies considerably from Shakespeare's, but Shakespeare was establishing a sense of foreboding. It is also probable that Shakespeare inserted this scene to establish the importance of the final battle, which is, of course, the climax of the play; he often made use of supernatural omens to foretell a tragic death, as, for example, in *Julius Caesar, Macbeth,* and *Hamlet.* Historians writing before and after Shakespeare's time often referred to such events, so it is difficult to know whether they did so because they believed that these events really occurred or because they were ingredients for a good story. At any rate, this scene creates a tense feeling of suspense. Our attention is focused wholly on this final battle, the one that will determine the fates of Caesar, Antony, and Cleopatra.

ACT IV – SCENE 4

Summary

It is early morning on the day of the great battle, and Cleopatra and some servants are helping Antony prepare for battle. Cleopatra urges him to sleep a bit longer, but Antony refuses; he calls for Eros, a servant, to bring him his armor. In a brief comic scene, Cleopatra says that *she* will help Antony put his armor on; she knows nothing about donning armor, of course, and so what she does is very clumsy. She picks up the wrong pieces, she buckles badly, but she eventually manages to get Antony dressed.

Trumpets sound offstage, soldiers enter, and Antony turns to Cleopatra and tenderly kisses her. He tells his men that the morning looks good, "like the spirit of a youth." He bids Cleopatra farewell, and he and his men exit. Cleopatra goes to her room to await the outcome.

Commentary

This fairly straightforward scene adds a momentary bit of lightness to the gloom of the preceding scene. The tender affection between Antony and Cleopatra is touching, for there is a sense of tragic irony here; we are familiar with the story, as were probably most of the theatergoers in Shakespeare's day. We know what the outcome will be. Still, however, there is a great deal of interest in seeing how the lovers' fates develop and how the dramatist will decide to create the tragedy's climax.

ACT IV – SCENE 5

Summary

At Antony's camp near Alexandria, a soldier brings word that Enobarbus, Antony's most trusted aide, has deserted and pledged his allegiance to Caesar's side. Moreover, Enobarbus fled in such haste that he left all his money and belongings behind. Antony is dismayed at Enobarbus's departure, but he honorably orders his former friend's belongings to be sent to him as a final gesture of friendship. Antony then tells Eros to write a letter to Enobarbus, saying in effect that Antony understands his actions and does not condemn him.

Commentary

Many of Antony's actions in this play display not only a generous spirit, but at times almost a prescient awareness that he will be a victim of fate. Rationally, he knows that his love for Cleopatra has changed his destiny. In Act I, Scene 2, he reflected that his dalliance with her caused him "ten thousand harms, I know." Yet love defies reason, and so, of course, it is additionally deeply demoralizing when Antony's "voice of reason," his trusted advisor, Enobarbus, loses faith and deserts him. Yet it is to Antony's credit that he does not suddenly become incensed and hate his old friend for this act.

ACT IV – SCENE 6

Summary

We now see Enobarbus at Caesar's camp as Caesar, Agrippa, and Dolabella plan for the coming battle. Caesar instructs his soldiers to place Antony's deserters on the front lines, presumably to demoralize Antony and his remaining men, for they will be unprepared for the psychological shock when they discover that they are fighting against their former comrades.

They all exit then, except Enobarbus, who contemplates his fate. He describes the fates of other deserters, especially Alexas, Cleopatra's confidential secretary. Alexas was followed, seized, and hanged. Obviously, Caesar is not welcoming Antony's deserters; they can expect little honor or trust at the hands of their new sovereign, but Enobarbus appears to be an exception.

A soldier enters to tell Enobarbus that Antony has sent "all thy treasure." Enobarbus doesn't believe him at first, and he is heartbroken when he realizes that the soldier has told the truth. He swears to himself that he cannot fight against such a noble-hearted general; his disgust with himself is so great that he vows to "go seek some ditch wherein to die."

Commentary

Antony's gesture of friendship to his old friend has tragic repercussions. Enobarbus is not grateful for his treasure; instead, he is remorseful about his decision to desert his former general. Because of Antony's trust in him and because of Enobarbus's reputation for honesty and integrity, Enobarbus is very respected by Caesar. But regardless of his treatment at Caesar's hands, Enobarbus has lost all sense of his own honor and integrity. It seems that there is nothing that can return these intangible qualities to him, unless he takes his life.

One should note here that in ancient Rome, and in other countries of the ancient world, suicide did not bear the stigma that it does now; then, it was often considered to be an honorable solution to many a problem. In particular, those whose lives might well be forfeited because they were conquered, or taken captive, often sought to end their lives rather than submit to the decrees of an enemy. Enobarbus's situation, however, is a bit different in that his resolve results from despair rather than from a fear of captivity or execution.

ACT IV – SCENE 7

Summary

This brief scene describes Antony's reaction to the battle that has begun. Apparently, Antony's forces are winning, although the odds were initially against it. Scarus, one of Antony's men, is badly wounded, but he bravely urges the rest of his men to continue the fight, "snatching them [the enemy] up like hares." Antony praises the soldier's valor, and he and his men leave to rejoin the battle.

Commentary

Here, we have another brief glimpse of Antony's impulsiveness and bravery. We also meet Scarus, a brave soldier who replaces Enobarbus, to some extent, as Antony's closest comrade. Unlike Enobarbus, however, whose intelligence and insight were useful to Antony precisely because he was calmer and more rational than his general, Scarus is very much like Antony. He is much more like a brave and faithful baying dog; he can be of great help to his master, but he cannot see beyond the immediate goal, nor look beyond the decisions of his master and predict consequences.

ACT IV – SCENE 8

Summary

The battle continues. Antony is next to the walls of Alexandria, and he tells his men to report to Cleopatra how well the battle is going. At that point, Cleopatra enters and greets them all. Antony takes Scarus's hand and presents him to Cleopatra. She congratulates him for his valor, and Antony embraces her. They are delighted with the battle's progress thus far, and they predict a complete victory by the next day. They leave then, preparing to celebrate that evening in anticipation of their victory.

Commentary

This scene has ironic overtones; Antony's preparations for his victory celebration are premature. In addition, his adoration for Cleopatra seems as changeable and unpredictable as the weather. Based on the earlier behavior of both lovers, we wonder when the next lapse in trust and the resulting quarrel between them will occur.

ACT IV – SCENE 9

Summary

The scene shifts briefly back to Caesar's camp. Sentries are keeping watch throughout the night, and they hear Enobarbus, still distraught, speaking to the moon. In a moving soliloquy, Enobarbus makes his final speech; he is a symbol of melancholy and madness, and he despairs that he deserted Antony. As he falls and dies, probably of self-inflicted wounds, the sentries go to him, thinking that he has merely fainted. When they discover that he is dead, they carry his body back to the camp.

Commentary

It is theatrically fitting that Enobarbus's final irrational despair and delirium should occur in a scene bathed in moonlight. Many people in Shakespeare's time believed that night air and moonlight could cause illness, depression, and even madness. Even now we have words based on such notions—"moonstruck," "lunatic," and "looney," for example. It is not clear from the stage instructions whether Enobarbus falls on his sword or whether he simply dies of self-inflicted wounds. Perhaps he has already stabbed himself, and we are hearing his last words. It is possible, however, that "the flint and hardness" of his fault is figurative only, and that he dies of grief and of a broken heart.

ACT IV – SCENE 10

Summary

On the battlefield, between the two camps, Antony and Scarus are conversing. Caesar was defeated on land yesterday, and they observe that he is now preparing for an attack on Antony by sea. Antony fearlessly states that wherever Caesar chooses to fight, he will fight him—whether on land, sea, fire, or air (the four elements of which the Elizabethans believed everything in the world to be made).

Commentary

Antony's bravery is somewhat emotionally exaggerated, but it is exactly right for his character and for his military strategy, for we have seen that for whatever reason, his forces do fare better on land than on sea. Thus his victory on land is not altogether a surprise. The battle at sea, however, is another matter. Antony is courageous, but he is not the careful tactician that Caesar is.

ACT IV—SCENE 11

Summary

We now return briefly to Caesar and his army, also on the battlefield. He instructs his men that unless they are attacked, they should keep their strongest forces on land, to hold the positions they have.

Commentary

Caesar's apparent sea preparations are a ruse. He hopes, by this maneuver, to draw off Antony's best men to sea and take advantage of this strategy on land, where, thus far, Antony has been the victor.

ACT IV—SCENE 12

Summary

Antony and Scarus watch the battle from a hill near Alexandria. Things are not going as well as Antony had hoped. From their position, they can see that the sea battle is lost and that Caesar has retained enough forces on land to continue the fight.

Antony leaves to find out how " 'tis like to go." He returns almost immediately and tells Scarus that they have lost. He believes that Cleopatra has betrayed him, and he curses her. She enters shortly thereafter, and he calls her a traitor and orders her away. Then he continues to rage, and he predicts that Cleopatra will die for her treachery.

Commentary

Antony's rage overpowers this scene. His accusations against Cleopatra seem especially unfair. We should remember, however, that in the past, Cleopatra has advised against (without luck) the use of sea power against Caesar. It is also likely here that Antony is remembering Caesar's earlier overtures to Cleopatra; it is also highly likely that bitter doubts arise again in his mind, regarding Cleopatra's loyalty and love.

ACT IV – SCENE 13

Summary

At the palace with her attendants, Cleopatra is confused by Antony's wrath; she does not understand his anger, and she tries one last scheme to see if she can win him back. Charmian has suggested that she go to her monument (the tomb which she has had built in the event of her death). There, she is to send word to Antony that she is dead; she instructs Mardian, the eunuch, to report to her how Antony reacts to this news.

Commentary

This is a dangerous ploy on Cleopatra's part, but she is desperate to dispel Antony's persistent doubts about her. Here we see the nature of the conflicts that have continually arisen between these two lovers. Cleopatra has always responded to adversity with a subtle scheme to circumvent its worst effects, if she can. This has made her seem more devious than perhaps she is; in fact, her response may be more of a cultural trait, part and parcel of life in an Oriental court, than it is a personal character trait. Antony, on the other hand, responds directly and impulsively to negative events; as a result, he frequently falls into the error of acting rashly and embroiling himself in unnecessary complications. Now, both Cleopatra

58

and Antony misjudge the other's motives – with tragic results, as we shall see shortly.

ACT IV – SCENE 14

Summary

Antony and Eros have returned to the palace, and Antony asks Eros if he can still *see* him. Eros doesn't understand the question, and so Antony explains; he describes himself as being like a shadow or a cloud, insubstantial yet taking on various shapes. He seems to be only a mere shadow of his former self because of his defeat by Caesar and because of what he assumes to be Cleopatra's treachery.

Mardian enters and tells Antony that Cleopatra ("My mistress [who] loved thee") is dead, and that the last words that she spoke were "Antony! most noble Antony!" Antony is horribly shocked and instantly regrets his mistrust of her. He vows that he too will end his life. He calls Eros and commands him to kill him. Eros hesitates, and Antony pleads with him, saying that surely Eros would not wish to see him a captive of Caesar, defeated and shamed. Eros agrees, and he asks Antony to turn the other way so that he will not see Eros's sword. Antony does so, and Eros kills himself instead, after saying farewell to Antony.

Antony, both abashed and impressed by Eros's courage and loyalty, follows his example and attempts to kill himself by falling upon his sword. Antony's sword, however, does not pierce him fatally. Hearing his cries, Dercetas and other soldiers enter, and although Antony begs them to kill him, no one will do so. Diomedes enters and finds Antony still alive. He tells Antony that Cleopatra has sent him word that she is, in fact, not dead – that she lives. He explains that Cleopatra had hoped to defuse his rage by sending him word of her death, but then she feared that he might take his life. Thus she has sent Diomedes to tell Antony the truth. Antony calls for his guards and tells them to take him to Cleopatra.

Commentary

We now see the results of Antony's poor judgment and mistrust. Having believed that he had lost everything, he attempted to kill himself, learning too late that he acted too rashly. Cleopatra, not fully understanding the agony of her Roman lover, precipitated his death by her melodramatic, manipulative playacting. (If this play is the first Shakespearean play one has seen, it may seem unreal that Antony takes so long to die; most people who stab themselves do not make long speeches about it. However, in opera and in Shakespeare's dramas, this is very often the case.)

ACT IV – SCENE 15

Summary

The scene opens at Cleopatra's monument, or tomb. Cleopatra is being comforted by her attendants when Diomedes enters to tell them what has happened to Antony. Shortly thereafter, Antony is carried in on a stretcher by his soldiers and is raised up to the balcony. There, he makes a farewell speech and bids Cleopatra to seek safety from Caesar. But Cleopatra refuses, and as Antony dies, she faints, mourning the loss of the only person who made her life worth living. She vows to bury him in Roman fashion, and, in addition, she vows to follow his example. As the scene ends, she and her women carry Antony's body away.

Commentary

Here we have proof that Cleopatra truly loved Antony. Yet we shall still see one last bit of her wily scheming as she deceives her Roman captors long enough to end her own life and follow Antony.

ACT V – SCENE 1

Summary

The final act opens at Caesar's camp in Alexandria. Dercetas enters with Antony's bloodied sword. Caesar is startled by the sight, and then Dercetas explains that this is the sword with which Antony killed himself. Caesar is affected by the irony of this moment, for while he fought hard for Antony's defeat or death, he is saddened by the fact that his rival is now dead, by his own hand. As he considers the tragedy of all that has happened, he speaks of Antony as being like his "brother," his "competitor," and his "mate in empire."

Like many of Shakespeare's great characters, Caesar speaks of men's fates as being determined by the stars. His and Antony's fates, he says, were ultimately "unreconcilable."

An Egyptian enters with a message from Cleopatra, asking for instructions from Caesar, the conqueror. Caesar promises kindness, and he sends Gallus and Proculeius to her with a message.

Commentary

Caesar's response to Antony's death evokes a reassessment and a new recognition of Antony's good qualities, his courage and sense of honor, which perhaps finally outweigh his faults. In this scene, we also note the unusual tenor of Cleopatra's letter, since the previous scene informed us that she intended to follow Antony into death. Obviously, she is planning something. Shakespeare's heroine remains a schemer to the end.

ACT V – SCENE 2

Summary

Back at her monument in Alexandria, Cleopatra and her attendants plan their immediate future. She does *not* intend to be taken alive by Caesar, however seemingly kind his intentions. Proculeius enters, and she remembers that Antony told her earlier that this man could be trusted. He asks what she would request from Caesar, and Cleopatra responds that she would like "conquered Egypt" for her son. Proculeius tells her not to worry, but to submit herself to Caesar and that she will be taken care of. Suddenly, however, soldiers enter and seize Cleopatra. She attempts to stab herself with a dagger but is disarmed. She vows, however, that she will die, somehow, before she will permit herself to be taken alive to Rome. She asks what Caesar plans to do with her and is told that she will be led as a captive into Rome.

Caesar and his party enter, and Caesar tells Cleopatra that if she does not resist him, she will be treated well; otherwise, he will have to use the same degree of force which he used against Antony. Cleopatra then gives Caesar a list of all her property, and she asks Seleucus, her treasurer, to affirm that the list is complete. He cannot swear to it, however, and states that it is not complete. Cleopatra admits to Caesar that she kept back a few "trifles," then turns on Seleucus, virtually accusing him of deception. He flees, and Caesar generously ignores this incident and tells Cleopatra to keep whatever she would like. He asks her not to consider herself a prisoner (although, in fact, she is one), and he leaves.

Cleopatra tells her ladies Iras and Charmian that Caesar's promises of friendship are empty; she whispers to Charmian to make preparations for her death according to their plan. An officer of Caesar, Dolabella, enters and tells Cleopatra that Caesar intends to send her and her children to Rome. He then takes his leave, and Cleopatra comments to Iras what their reception in Rome is likely to be like. There, she predicts, they will be dragged through town like whores, and amateur actors will put on cheap plays portraying Antony as a drunk and portraying her as a harlot.

When Charmian enters, Cleopatra tells her attendants to fetch her best clothing so that she may be properly dressed to meet Antony. A guard enters and tells Cleopatra that some "rural fellow" has arrived with a basket of figs for her; she tells him to permit the man to enter. The peasant enters, carrying a covered basket that contains poisonous asps. Cleopatra asks him about the nature of the "worm of Nilus," meaning the asp, and he tells her how dangerous it is. He warns her to be careful in handling it. It is not clear whether or not he realizes how she intends to use it, but as he leaves, he says, "I wish you all joy of the worm," a heavily ironic statement.

Iras enters with Cleopatra's robe and crown, and Cleopatra puts them on and makes her farewells. She kisses Iras and Charmian, and Iras falls dead, unexplainably, at her feet.

Cleopatra and Charmian are both grieved at Iras's death, but Cleopatra resolutely places an asp upon her breast. Charmian protests, but it is too late. The Egyptian queen lets another asp bite her arm, and she dies, saying that soon she will be with Antony.

A guard enters, and Charmian tells him not to wake Cleopatra. He says that Caesar has sent a message, but she interrupts and says that Caesar sent "too slow a messenger." Charmian then kills herself with an asp.

By this time, the guards call for Dolabella. He enters and confirms that what Caesar feared has happened. Caesar enters then and discovers that Cleopatra and her women are dead. While it frustrates his purposes, he respects her integrity, perhaps for the first time in the play.

> Bravest at the last!
> She levell'd at our purposes, and, being royal,
> Took her own way.
>
> (339-41)

They are all puzzled as to the cause of her death until they discover the asp bites. Caesar again is impressed with her devotion and integrity, and he vows to see her buried in a fitting manner:

> Take up her bed,
> And bear her women from the monument.
> She shall be buried by her Antony.
> No grave upon earth shall clip in it
> A pair so famous.
>
> (359-63)

Commentary

In this final scene, Cleopatra meets with Caesar's representatives and cleverly feigns that she is interested in continuing her life; she attempts to negotiate with the Romans and even offers Caesar a list of her property (with the exception of certain secret items that she would need; it is possible, of course, that Seleucus was privy to this plan in order to make Cleopatra's act all the more convincing). Realistically, of course, if we can believe Cleopatra, she has no need to retain any of her property, for ostensibly she plans to commit suicide, like Antony. What we see in her final actions, then, is her characteristic manner of facing difficult situations. Of necessity, Cleopatra schemes and playacts one last time; thus, by her very coyness, her childish quality becomes, ironically, the means by which she maintains her loyalty to Antony. What was once a game for her now becomes a weapon and enables her to prolong her life long enough to defy Caesar himself.

Caesar is the military victor, but the final scene suggests that he is ultimately no victor. He lacks something of the larger-than-life humanity of Antony and Cleopatra. Yet Shakespeare does not falsely idealize the lovers either. Their faults are visible to the end, but they do not overshadow the lovers' honor. If there is any ultimate character flaw in this play, it is one that all three of the main figures possess: lack of proportion. Caesar single-mindedly pursues power and, as a result, he seems too often to be merely a cold and calculating person. Antony and Cleopatra exalt love above their responsibilities; their respective realms, as a result, suffer. Cleopatra is particularly self-indulgent, preferring to play games with Antony while war develops almost at her doorstep. Antony, in contrast to both Cleopatra and Caesar, is never consistently a Roman *nor* an Egyptian. His vacillation about his duty and about his love ultimately results in his downfall.

CHARACTER ANALYSES

Antony

Antony, like Julius Caesar, is descended from an ancient Roman family, though lately the family has fallen into disfavor. Antony seems to have been a rather worthless person in his youth; he liked to drink too much, and he tended to be a spendthrift. He continued to exhibit these qualities for the rest of his life. But he also has a generous nature and a good-humored personality, and eventually he becomes a lieutenant to Julius Caesar in Gaul. His troops like him, and he is courageous on the battlefield. He becomes a chief deputy to Caesar, and eventually he is a partner with him as consul in Rome.

Antony makes his "second home" in the mysterious East, in Egypt, the civilization of the Ptolemies, in the play. Rome seems cold and grey, whereas Alexandria shimmers with heat and sparkles with color and sensuality. Antony's personality is much like the land where he makes his home in his middle years.

Antony seems to have acquired a new interest in the pleasures of living because of his residing in Egypt and because of his love for Cleopatra. Finally, however, he becomes a very troubled man because he found himself torn between a desire to be with Cleopatra and an equally strong desire to seek and maintain power in Rome.

His impulsiveness and his inability to make decisions make him appear weak, but he is not as weak as he appears, as the play illustrates. He is sensual, but he is also brave, and he withstands adversity well. He is insecure about his age, to some extent, for he worries about Cleopatra's fidelity, since he is older than she is. But in spite of his insecurities, Antony more often than not is overconfident.

He seriously underestimates his youthful opponent, Octavius Caesar; he believes that his own vast experience and courage on the field can make up for Octavius's inexperienced determination. He finds ultimately that they do not. Antony is finally driven to make a choice between his allegiance to Egypt and Cleopatra—or to Rome; he must declare his allegiance to one world or the other. He cannot have both, and it becomes clear early in the play that Rome's problems demand his full loyalty, rather than half. Antony's failure to see the nature of his problem causes him to endlessly vacillate, avoiding making a final decision until it is too late. Much of Antony's apparent impulsiveness, first deciding to give up all for Cleopatra, then deciding to return to Rome, etc., is a direct result of his basic underlying indecision. Because he cannot come to a conclusion about what values take precedence in his life, he loses everything.

One of his first mistakes is letting himself be drawn into the world of Egypt and its delights. He forgets that not all Romans conceive of Egypt as he does. He loses much popular support, due in large part to Octavius Caesar's criticism; thus, ultimately, his devotion to Cleopatra seems like disloyalty to Rome. Yet, despite all his mistakes, Antony is a heroic figure, drawn larger than life by Shakespeare's poetry. His ever-increasing indecision is the mirror of his inner struggle to find a balance between two worlds and two sets of values. If he fails, it isn't because he doesn't try to achieve all that he can. His adventurous attitude suggests that he attempts to enlarge his awareness of what life can be. By contrast, Octavius is not heroic simply because he never questions his ideals nor deeply weighs his loyalties. Audiences, readers, and critics have always disagreed as to whether or not Antony made the right choice. Perceptions of the meaning of his actions will differ, but the end result is the same: *Antony and Cleopatra* is a powerful play because it has powerful characters who catch the imagination and never release it. They are lovers who are more mature than Romeo and Juliet and, for that reason, they are not easily forgotten.

Cleopatra

If an imaginary spectrum were constructed and if Octavius Caesar were placed at one end of the spectrum, Antony would waver, swaying and shifting in the middle, and Cleopatra would be found at the other end of the spectrum. Not only is she Queen of Egypt, she is the epitome of Egypt itself. She represents all those qualities that Octavius and the practical Romans have denied themselves – enjoyment, playfulness, sensuality, and passion. But like all the other major characters, Cleopatra is more than an allegory of personality traits. She is a full-dimensional, complex human being. In his portrayal of this woman, Shakespeare has taken the view of her as presented in countless legends and blended in many subtler features. She is no longer the one-dimensional, near-mythical queen of a mysterious and erotic country.

Cleopatra is a monarch, but we rarely see her performing any of the functions of one. She meets Antony, falls in love with him, and she appears to be totally devoted to pleasure and to finding fulfillment through her relationship with him. Her love for Antony becomes, ultimately, the most important thing in her life. But the strength of her passion is hidden by the superficial mannerisms which she uses to manipulate people, so that initially in the play, the impression that the audience has of her is simplistic – that is, it is consistent with the stereotype of the Egyptian harlot-queen. Later, Shakespeare transforms her into a complex, confused woman. Tragically, Cleopatra never realizes that the games which she plays to gain attention are often misinterpreted by Antony; yet it is clear that she is devoted to him – more than even he is to her, at first. Nor does she betray him at the end in order to bargain for her own life. One reason for her continual playacting with Antony is that she is basically an insecure woman. Initially, she would like Antony to marry her, but he is married to Fulvia. When Fulvia dies, Antony is almost immediately married to Octavius's sister, Octavia, in order to cement a political truce recently formed between himself and his rival, Octavius Caesar. Cleopatra fears that if she were Antony's wife, he would treat her in as cavalier a manner as he has his other women, for he willingly abandons them to spend time with her.

One important thing to note about Cleopatra throughout the play is her technique of subterfuge which she employs to get her way: all her ploys are part and parcel of the culture she lives in, the "mysterious East" which has long been symbolized for Westerners by indirection and pretense. Audiences don't often realize this fact until the end of the play, but Cleopatra's manner never affects her essential integrity. It is yet one more illusion in a country known for illusion and mystery to Shakespeare's audience.

Octavius Caesar

In Julius Caesar's will, his grand-nephew, Octavius, was named as his heir and adoptive son. Octavius was related to Caesar through his grandfather, who married a sister of the Roman dictator.

As one of the three triumvirs, Octavius is the youngest and the most ambitious of the three. He began his career with little — except the name of his grand-uncle Julius Caesar, his father by adoption, and he naturally wanted more — all that was possible. Having been named heir in Caesar's will, Octavius comes to Rome to claim his fortune.

Nothing exists for young Caesar except the single goal of acquiring and maintaining power. As such, he is the antithesis of Antony, who becomes involved in a love affair that ultimately outweighs his own quest for mastery of the world. Because of the limited range of Octavius's vision and interests, he often appears cold and calculating, and many of his actions are indeed calculated ones. In betrothing his beloved sister to Antony, his long-time rival, he shows that he is capable of placing political expediency above family loyalty. Conversely, when Antony abandons Octavia, Octavius acts like the outraged brother who wishes to avenge his sister's honor. While his pride is understandably piqued, his anger also hints of opportunism, for here is the perfect pretext for attacking his rival.

Octavius struggles for supremacy within the Triumvirate, but interestingly, his contest is only with Antony, for neither he nor Antony considers Lepidus an equal. Throughout the drama, neither Antony nor Octavius trusts the other. Nor does Octavius's sister, Octavia, wholly trust Antony. She is well aware of his greater experience in battle and statesmanship, as well as his popularity with his soldiers and with the public, compared to her brother's inexperience. Quite naturally, Octavius is insecure about his ability to succeed in an arena where Antony has been active for close to twenty years. But he gains confidence as he observes Antony's dissipated life in Egypt, and he takes advantage of every situation he can.

Octavius has few devoted friends, and Shakespeare seemingly uses him to illustrate the lot of the ruler who must sacrifice everything to stay in power. He trusts no one, and he fears to let himself be close to few, if any, of his men. His treatment of Lepidus is one example of how he can cast aside presumed friends in order to achieve even more power. It is possible, of course, that Antony might have treated Lepidus unfairly, but in fact, it was Octavius who imprisoned the third member of the Triumvirate and confiscated his lands. Octavius, at times, seems almost without principle. For example, one of Octavius's closest friends, his officer Dolabella, surreptitiously helps Cleopatra by warning her that Octavius plans to take her to Rome in disgrace if she is captured. Cleopatra is thus able to thwart Octavius's devious schemes. She takes her own life and thus deprives him of parading her through the streets of Rome in disgrace–all for the glory of Octavius, the conqueror. Basically, then, we can say that Octavius symbolizes the world of power, politics, and war. The Rome of this play is the Rome of the waning Republic. It is a masculine, taciturn, and seemingly pleasureless place: fittingly, it is the seat of Octavius's realm.

While Octavius's character often seems pale in comparison with Shakespeare's portraits of Antony and Cleopatra, he is vital to the play, for he functions both as Antony's antagonist and as his foil. Without the dour young Octavius as a rival and as a contrast, Antony's virtues, as well as his faults, would not be so vividly apparent for the audience–nor for Cleopatra, for that matter.

Lepidus

Lepidus became one of the triumvirs partly because he had a large number of soldiers under his command and also because Antony needed him. He served to balance the power of Antony and young Octavius Caesar, because he was a threat to neither Octavius nor Antony.

Lepidus is the eldest of the three men, and he is, perhaps, the least ambitious. It is possible for that very reason that Antony and Octavius are able to dominate him and make his position in the Triumvirate largely that of a figurehead.

The real Lepidus undoubtedly was not the buffoon which he appears to be in this play, but his lack of actual power is fairly accurate. He serves as both a foil and a mediator for the more powerful triumvirs, who are rivals for the ultimate prize of the Roman Empire.

Enobarbus

Enobarbus is Antony's most devoted friend; he is so loyal and so trusted, in fact, that he is able to comment freely, even when he feels critical of Antony. And he has much to be critical of, for he can reason in situations when Antony's sense of reason deserts him. When Antony is torn by indecision, Enobarbus speaks up; he says what he feels should be done and, most important, he is not blinded, as Antony is, by an all-consuming infatuation with Cleopatra.

Enobarbus often serves the function of the commentator. He can move about freely, he sees much that occurs among the heads of state, and thus he forms his own conclusions, which he shares with his comrades and the audience. He is a cynic of sorts, whom neither power nor love impresses. His only mistake, seemingly, is in deserting Antony when it becomes clear Antony will lose the war. Not surprisingly, Antony's generosity to his former friend so shames him that he takes his own life.

QUESTIONS FOR REVIEW

1. What qualities do you think are most dominant in the characters of (1) Antony; (2) Cleopatra; and (3) Octavius Caesar? Which character do you admire the most? Why? Which character do you dislike the most? Why?

2. Do you think that any of the characters in this play could be described as a hero or a villain? Why or why not?

3. What value systems do the two countries of Rome and Egypt appear to represent?

4. What role do you think Enobarbus plays in the relationship between Antony and Cleopatra, and between Antony and the other triumvirs?

5. Does Shakespeare, in your opinion, value more the goals of Octavius Caesar or those of Antony? Why?

6. Discuss the dominant images in this play. For example, discuss the imagery of the world, of vastness, of the heavens, and explain how Shakespeare uses them to create characters who are larger than life.

7. Which emotion dominates in Antony and Cleopatra's relationship? Is it love or lust? Explain your choice.

8. Discuss Shakespeare's use of the images of heat and sunlight and how they are used in relation to the themes of love and war.

9. Discuss Shakespeare's attitudes towards sex and love as they are illustrated in this play. How are they similar to current ideas? How do they differ? Also compare the comic scenes with Cleopatra's servants with some of the more serious scenes between Antony and Cleopatra.

10. Consider in depth any one of the three main characters. Examine how that character is viewed by the others in the play and by Shakespeare's audience.

SELECTED BIBLIOGRAPHY

ADAMS, J. Q. *A Life of William Shakespeare.* Boston: Houghton Mifflin Co., 1923.

ALEXANDER, PETER. *Shakespeare.* Oxford: Oxford University Press, 1964.

BEVINGTON, DAVID. *Shakespeare.* Arlington Heights, Ill.: A.H.M. Publications, 1978.

BLOOM, EDWARD A., ed. *Shakespeare 1564-1964.* Providence: Brown University Press, 1964.

BRADLEY, A. C. *Shakespearean Tragedy.* London: The Macmillan Co., 1904.

CHARLTON, H. B. *Shakespearean Tragedy.* Cambridge, England: Cambridge University Press, 1948.

CRAIG, HARDIN. "The Great Trio," *An Interpretation of Shakespeare.* Columbia, Missouri: Lucas Brothers, 1966.

FARNHAM, WILLARD. *The Medieval Heritage of Elizabethan Tragedy.* Berkeley, California: University of California Press, 1936.

GIBSON, H. N. *The Shakespeare Claimants.* New York: Barnes & Noble, Inc., 1962.

HEILMAN, ROBERT B. *Magic in the Web.* Lexington, Kentucky: University of Kentucky Press, 1956.

KNIGHT, G. WILSON. *The Wheel of Fire.* London: Oxford University Press, 1930.

LEAVIS, F. R. *The Common Pursuit.* Hardmonsworth, Middlesex: Penguin Books, Ltd., 1963.

RIBNER, IRVING. *Patterns in Shakespearean Tragedy.* New York: Barnes & Noble, Inc., 1960.

SEWELL, ARTHUR. *Character and Society in Shakespeare.* Oxford: Clarendon Press, 1951.

SPIVACK, BERNARD. *Shakespeare and the Allegory of Evil.* New York: Columbia University Press, 1958.

STIRLING, BRENTS. *Unity in Shakespearean Tragedy: The Interplay of Theme and Character.* New York: Columbia University Press, 1956.

NOTES

NOTES